Draw My Heart
After You
in the
Song of Love

Virginia Helweg

CREATION HOUSE
A Strang Company

DRAW MY HEART AFTER YOU IN THE SONG OF LOVE
   by Virginia Helweg
Published by Creation House
A Strang Company
600 Rinehart Road
Lake Mary, Florida 32746
www.strangbookgroup.com

Design Director: Bill Johnson

Cover design by Nathan Morgan

Library of Congress Control Number: 2010931343
International Standard Book Number: 978-1-61638-212-4

First Edition

10 11 12 13 14 — 9 8 7 6 5 4 3 2 1
Printed in the United States of America

Contents

Acknowledgments

*I*N THE LATE '50s I walked off the stage of the largest nightclub in the world in Hollywood, California. I was wearing a beautiful costume, a tall feather hat, and stage make-up. I was then a UCLA student and worked at the Moulin Rouge at night to pay my way through college. Plus I was having fun! I caught a glimpse of myself in a full-length mirror, and in a cocky spirit I asked myself, "What is the best thing that has ever happened to you thus far in life?" Right then the presence of the Living God surrounded me. It was not a vision but a presence, and I knew the answer was He! I left the show four months later and joined Hollywood Presbyterian Church. I worked with Dr. Henrietta Mears.

A couple of years later she hired an engineer who had just left the navy to attend Fuller Seminary. He was to fix all of the audiovisual equipment plus run a Wednesday night group for junior high kids. She told him to get a woman helper. He was not pleased with this. He had overseen 200 men in the navy, and he did not need a woman leader. He made this plain to Dr. Mears, but she was insistent! I now entered the scene. After a couple of years of marriage, I asked about this and why he asked me to help him. If he had to have a woman assistant, then she might as well have pretty legs!

Otto was the best supporter in my life to stay on task in writing this book. His strength was a great blessing to me throughout our forty-four years of marriage. He is now full of the joy of heaven. God took him home November 2, 2008. He left me with three great sons who are all professional men and take great care of their mother. I am also blessed with two wonderful daughters-in-law plus two beautiful granddaughters.

God has surrounded me with other friends such as Kay Lewis, a pastor's wife, and Collette Michaels who has established a foreign student ministry at North Dakota State University. Both of these women have lovingly given me great encouragement in the writing of this book. Glen and Pat Doughty have encouraged and supported Otto and me all of our lives. They allowed us to spend our honeymoon in their home. This was a great blessing, for we were broke and leaving for Iran in a few weeks. Pat calls me once a month to see if I am working on this book. Dough and Merry Steward have been very close to us throughout our lives. Otto and Dough were classmates at the Naval Academy and again at Fuller Seminary. He was the only who could keep Otto and me on the straight and narrow! We always loved having them in our home. There have also been many others who encouraged us in our faith. God has been fully faithful to us throughout our lives!

Introduction

FATHER GOD SINGS to us through the music of this special song. Its melodies, directed to our hearts, will birth within us the bride of Christ. The Holy Spirit knows how to engage its sweet harmonies to intertwine them in the very fabric of our beings. We move closer to Him as the least likely candidates for this wonderful transformation. As we are, could we ever be chosen as His bride, the bride of Christ?

Don't we all hunger for someone to love us passionately within the context of all our failures and flaws. Personal love is that grandiose failure we experience throughout our lifetimes. Love fails, sometimes partially, but more within the human experience.

Along with the Gospels, The Song of Songs reveals to us unfailing love—personal, kissing love, directed into the humanity of broken lives.

How serious is the living God in loving me? He has so many wounded hearts that desperately need His quality of healing love. Most of us are deeply damaged either through our own stubborn choices in life, or simply through the same choices made by those closest to us. The common human experience is this, but unfortunately the common human elixir we select, is not the living God. However His love is far more than medicinal. His loving presence fully satisfies the wounded heart.

But I'm junk! How could God ever genuinely love me? I am desperately lost and so often discarded by those closest to me.

He's the master at loving junk. His love transcends all the personal problems you and I bring to Him. He easily finds you, no matter where you are. You lost Him but He never lost you. He's a tenacious lover. You run and hide, but He will find you because in His heart He refuses to lose you.

The first voice in the Song in chapter one verse two is that of a forced field laborer. It's the voice from a damaged heart, and throughout The Song we will follow this heartbeat into glorious wholeness.

When we choose to move in God's desire and into His fullness, we then flow into His enormous reservoir of life. Our energies collapse in Him washed in utter joy—full personal knowledge bathed in His passion. A quality of knowledge He desires to impart within us as the temples of His magnificent presence. This describes this special journey.

As common people what do we truly know of Him? We have mostly scattered thoughts and feelings. "The Song of Songs, which is Solomon's" (1:1), describes this unusual journey of the heart into worship as our spirit, soul, and body become functioning tabernacles of God's personal pleasure.

We are not simply to know something about God. Our special subject matter may never be reduced to truth as only facts, or ink. Knowledge concerning Him is not simply studying history, as helpful as that may be. Knowledge in Him requires personal intimacy of heart and soul. The Song pulls us precisely into that direction.

Do we at all grasp the depth of who we are within the confines of our hearts? One of the most common icons used by our culture is the heart. We use it everywhere—on candy wrappers, movie posters, for everything from candy to cars. And yet the human heart is profoundly for Him, the living God. Then, The Song is essentially about giddy emotionalism? Never! Not at all! What takes place within us when God fully wins our hearts? The full substance of the bride of Christ is born.

Perhaps we do exist light years away from any perception of who we truly are in the depths of our being—created in the image of God, and chosen to experience His Bridegroom love.

What should I understand? What will I grasp as to its importance to my general well-being and to my future? I don't know. But I do believe that our personal theology of the living God will change dramatically. His kisses within the heart and soul have a tendency to do this—all the knowledge we now possess of Him wrapped within kissing intimacy.

Wow, He's after our hearts! He pursues within us heart-level intercourse. This knowledge does not always satisfy the mind, nor is it easily explained by the mind; but is authentically known in the heart. The poetic metaphors of The Song teach us that this level of knowledge will be known within us; not necessarily because of who we are, but because we were created in His image and therefore have an inbuilt capacity to know Him intimately, as in marriage love.

Does this book give the last word on intimacy with the living God? Not at all! I know I have simply skimmed the surface. Not because those were my intentions, but more because of my own spiritual journey. Use this book to write out and record what your heart enjoys in Him and grow in love.

Where does it begin? First, it begins with new birth through the sacrifice of Jesus Christ our Savior. He died for all our sins and restores us, just as we are, to His Father. And that's it?

Absolutely not! We now enter the journey into intimacy with the Bridegroom, Lover of our souls. Is The Song essentially about romantic love? Yes, but never as we have ever perceived romance on the human level.

The Song of Songs is so unusual because it is a love poem framed as a song. This is most appropriate because we are a singing, praising, and worshiping faith. King Solomon grew up in an atmosphere of incredible worship. He was a writer of songs as was David, his father. Solomon wrote 1,005 songs, and this is the only one we have today.

I believe his life was profoundly influenced by David's tabernacle where it is thought that worship was evident twenty-four hours a day for several decades. I believe this life dynamic birthed The Song of Songs within Solomon's heart. God established him as the most glorious king of his day, which reflects the glory of Christ as the King of kings. We are not being chosen by a "loser."

There are two important voices in the singing of The Song. The first voice is that of a woman whose heart is seeking the presence of this glorious king, and the other voice is that of a most delighted king. The other voices are those of traveling spectators who discern through the woman's experiences that something marvelous is taking place within her. They are held captive to know what or who it is.

The woman journeys forth from her roots in the dark tents which created distance within her from the living God. Who does she represent? None other than the human heart. Who does he represent? The King of kings, the Lord Jesus Christ.

In the Book of Hebrews we are exhorted to "draw near" six times. In the New Testament this book corresponds to The Song. And to what do we draw near? To the One who has come as close as possible to His people in the fullness of His present glory. The Holy Spirit draws us in through His blood and into His presence, not as strangers, but as lovers, His bride. The Song will teach us about this sublime journey of the heart and soul. It's intended to be deeply personal. He takes liberties.

What form of wisdom and knowledge could the poetry of this song offer to us? Not historical, not prophetic, not necessarily the everyday practical teaching we are in such need of.

The Song births beautiful personal journeys. His passion for each of us is overwhelming! He knows my name and He knows everything about me, and yet He still pursues me as only a committed lover can.

May The Song be a blessing to you as it has been to me. I have written this small book not as a commentary, for there are many excellent ones available today, but as a devotional book. May it draw you into a deeper revelation of the Lover of your soul, who gave everything to make this intimacy a personal reality.

> *Oh, Lover of our souls, The Song is not so much about what You do for us, but more as to who You are within us. How is it you hunger so for Your people when we live out our lives in overall complacency towards You?*
>
> *What is it about me that You long for my presence? There is no one who desires me as much as You do. How is*

*it that you will not let me go when holding on to you plays
such a small part within me? Oh, teach me the magnificent
ways of your heart.*

Watchman Nee in his book of the same title says the following:

> The Song of Songs which is Solomon's; Solomon
> composed a thousand and five songs (1 Kings 4:32).
> Of all these songs, this by far is the most excellent, and
> consequently it is spoken of as "The Song of Songs." The
> most holy place in the tabernacle is called "the holy of
> holies." After the same style the Lord Jesus is called "the
> King of kings, and Lord of lords." This in like manner is
> "The Song of Songs."
>
> The Book of Ecclesiastes, which precedes it, is an
> exposition of the vanity of vanities while this, in contrast,
> is "The Song of Songs." The song which is Solomon's,
> therefore, is the antithesis of what is represented by
> the Book of Ecclesiastes. Ecclesiastes speaks of a life of
> wandering. The Song speaks of rest from wandering.
> Ecclesiastes tells us that one cannot obtain satisfaction
> through knowledge alone. The Song tells us that man
> can reach satisfaction only through love.
>
> Again, Ecclesiastes relates the pursuit of all things
> under the sun. The Song relates specifically to the
> pursuit of things in Christ. In Ecclesiastes we find that
> the wrong things are sought for and the ways of seeking
> them are wrong, resulting in the conviction that all
> under the sun is "vanity of vanities." But that which is
> sought after in The Song of Solomon is the right thing
> and the way is right. Therefore the consummation is the
> supreme blessedness.[1]

The Song of Songs has been interpreted in a number of ways. The
fact that its truth is found in poetic metaphor allows for this.

- The love of Jehovah for Israel: "Thy maker is thy husband," (Isaiah 54:5); Israel is called to be His chosen bride.

- The love of Christ for His church as seen in Ephesians 5: "Husbands love your wives as Christ loved the church and gave himself up for her" (v. 25).

- God's great love for His children and the individual believer. Paul defines faith in this way: "I have been crucified with Christ; it is no longer I who live, but Christ lives in me; and the life which I now live in the flesh I live by faith in the Son of God, who loved me and gave Himself for me" (Gal. 2:20, NKJV). Paul's definition of his relationship in Christ is married love. The covenant union between a man and a woman mirrors our union with Christ as his chosen bride body, soul, and spirit.

Commentaries have suggested that The Song is written as several complete songs within themselves. A song ends and there is a passage of time. Then the next song continues to teach us the next phase of the divine relationship Christ has with His church.

I have been comfortable with the following divisions.

Song One   1:2–2:7
Song Two   2:8–3:5
Song Three   3:6–5:9
Song Four   5:10–8:3
Song Five   8:4–14

All the scripture used in this book is from the RSV translation unless otherwise noted.

Song One

Chamber Love

1:2–2:7

*T*HE HUMAN HEART is always seeking to be authentically loved, body, soul, and spirit. Our personal life journeys attest to this. The journey in The Song introduces us to the heart of the living God through poetic synthesis. So then it slides us into pure emotionalism? Nonsense! It connects us, in the deepest possible ways, into a personal knowledge that His loving intimacy fully desires you and me, just as we are. He hungers for our attentive presence. Nowadays what's the knowledge of the living God within our hearts really worth? Everything!

What's this song about? It's about the sublime adventure birthed within the human heart. Not simply a momentary delight, but a relationship. We need and desire so much more! We cry out to experience heaven's value of us! Nearly everything in our world cheapens who we are.

We thirst for someone to show us why we were ever created. And is there anyone who truly desires us? We need a lover with the tenacity to fulfill these needs. We need a very special lover. But, honestly, who hungers the most for this relationship? The Song teaches us that it's God who hungers the most.

As earth wanderers we miss the mark over and over again. We know intuitively we are not the people we were destined to become. All our lives we have received grades telling us of our worth, whether

1

in school or within social contacts or within our family's expectations. We know something deep and wonderful is missing within us. This song, heaven's song, speaks profoundly to our hearts concerning these things. These words are not essentially words, but more His divine presence.

The secret of fully living, or living fully, is never directed towards *something* but rather to *Someone*—a truth we easily miss. And we were never destined to simply know something about this Someone.

Wham! Bang! This song confronts us with the more—King of kings and Lord of lords, and still far more—the Bridegroom of the human heart. The living God wants a bride for His Son, and He's chosen you and me!

Now to get our attention: we understand He wants to save us, and graciously has. But now the pursuit: not necessarily our persistence, but more His. God is intent on birthing this bride within the human heart.

Lead us into the knowledge of your presence.

It will not be a general pulpit relationship where I am casually somewhere within a large audience. This does not satisfy His heart concerning you and me.

The Song begins the unfolding of these truths through the voice of a most unlikely candidate. She is the speaker in the first seven verses in Song One. She approaches this beautiful king with three outcries of her heart. Her heart and soul is the product of the dark tents of life.

In studying this soul, I complained to the Lord that she was not a real person, never flesh and blood. She's nothing but poetry. I wanted to study a real person, because I'm that person. God answered, "I have created this heart and soul to teach you of your pilgrimage in Me. Her words are My words."

"Oh let him kiss me with the kisses of his mouth" (1:2)

Who is saying this? A deeply wounded heart and soul. Someone no one wants to kiss. Someone who's an interior mess and who is no one's love or joy. One stuck in the fields of life.

How presumptuous she is in pressing in face-to-face with this king. But the truth is, though she is speaking these words, the living God inspired them. Her words are His words.

This book is not history. It is poetry birthed within the heart of a glorious King who represents this Lover of our souls, King Jesus. But surely scripture does not begin like this. What is God thinking? "Kisses of his mouth?"

He says, "Your whole world is intimate within you, body, soul, and spirit, and I'm not. Revelation of Me and My Bridegroom Son is directed towards you, and within you. The bride of Christ is entirely My desire for you. I've chosen you. I now wait for you to fully choose Me."

This book defines His kisses within our hearts and soul. Personal kisses blessing us into His glory. His kisses and His anointing upon and within us, drawing us into a love life we never experienced before.

> *Kiss my eyes to receive this revelation. Kiss my ears that I might truly know You in every dimension of my life. Your kisses reveal how close You are to me. Allow my ears to be antennas to Your abiding presence. And kiss my mouth that I will declare your beauty and Your faithfulness within me.*

He fully understands us. The human heart is a delicate mechanism which is easily defiled, damaged, and broken. If we have ever said to ourselves in enormous frustration, "What's wrong with you? You've blown it again! Can't you do anything right?" Then we, above anyone else, have personal heart problems.

He cries out for this form of revelation to daily fill our hearts— loving, kissing intimacy with the living God and His Son. I am not aware of this expression anywhere else in Scriptures. For this reason it has remained an enigma to me. But after years of thinking about these opening words to The Song of Songs, I've come to wholeheartedly believe how much I need His quality of loving and this feature of His presence within me.

That which is beautiful here is the Father's heart, which not only inspired these words, but can hardly wait to answer this unlikely outcry of her heart. He never rejected her and to Him she was never lost. He has always been waiting for her to simply respond, "Please kiss me with the kisses of Your mouth."

> But Lord, it's so difficult to comprehend this quality of loving. Kisses are cheap to me, and there are now too many walls between us.

So, meet the wall leaper. He says, "Nothing will stand between us in my fully loving you, no matter what your heart condition may be." The Bridegroom in this relationship said this to His Father:

> Lo, I have come to do thy will.' He abolishes the first in
> order to establish the second. And by that will we have
> been sanctified through the offering of the body of Jesus
> Christ once for all.
>
> —Hebrews 10:9–10

The Bridegroom has done this for us. He makes us ready to enter into the holy of holies. But what we have not understood is that He has already chosen us. Now He waits.

"Kiss me with the kisses of his mouth" (1:2)

> You are not the God of rules as the Pharisees were, which
> gave them control over lives.

God allows us to fulfill His law through His abiding love. He has never simply been ink, but more of a glorious life presence.

But what form of presence? King and Lord, most definitely, yes! But there is more about His presence which may puzzle us; for there is also the heart of a Bridegroom who is the intimate Lover of the heart and soul. If we never choose to know the Savior, then our hearts within us die a long, slow death.

In quietness He waits and draws us to Himself. Perhaps all we ever receive is a sense of the fullness of who He is. But wow! He is capturing our hearts, and we are growing in the knowledge of the living God...within His sweet presence.

> Thou dost show me the path of life; in thy presence there is fullness of joy, in thy right hand are pleasures for evermore.
>
> —PSALM 16:11

Romance my heart into a silence which embraces your beauty and your fullness of life and joy. Train and teach me to radically know you in this sweet bond. This knowledge fills me with your beauty, strength, and holiness.

In utter ignorance and internal emptiness we live out our days, never knowing nor experiencing His personal love. Yet, we are created and destined for this unusual romance of the human heart.

(See Psalms 21:6, 31:20, 42:8; Isaiah 55:8.)

"Oh let him kiss me with the kisses of his mouth" (1:2)

There is a "love life" appointed unto our personal lives. Why? Because these kisses belong to the one who has given everything to release authentic love into our hearts and souls. This love is essentially a person who is called Bridegroom of the heart and soul. The relationship is already established. I don't have to beg, "Choose me! Love me intimately! Please want me!" Most of us have only experienced the imitation. But He's the real thing!

Our faith is created for this intimacy with the Son, appointed the Bridegroom of the human heart by His Father. This relationship has already been established long before our personal lives entered into this world. In God's mind the only appropriate way to start this song is with His kisses of His mouth.

We need a paradigm shift concerning our relationship with the living God. He never desired that our relationship in Him would essentially be tied to a pew a couple of hours a week or month. These first words, "kisses of His mouth," offend me. They don't fit into my religion; my concept of the living God.

Must we make these kisses such an issue? Yes, because He is! This book is about these kisses from the heavenly Father on our lives. Personal kisses blessing us into His glory; His kisses and His anointing. This is describing a whole new quality of knowledge in the living God. This is a paradigm shift for most of us.

He's says to us, "Desire my kisses. You've lived out your life knowing the kisses of so many false lovers. It's now time to experience Mine. But first you must ask. My love is a gentleman's love. I will never coerce you! But beware; one kiss will never be enough! I want you closer to Me. I will continue to pursue you throughout your life."

How does this fit into my theology? It doesn't. These kisses are about Bridegroom love, directed precisely into my undernourished soul. All my life I have cried out for an authentic love life. And all this time He's been so close to me.

This book is not about emotionalism. It is about creating within us an authentic love life which develops into genuine worship. It is about satisfying the Father's heart in building within each of us the personal knowledge of the Lover of our soul. Quietly, beautifully He kisses me.

Drawing His people into this knowledge of intimacy with the living God may be the most important theme in The Song. He longs to saturate the heart with the intimacy of His presence and His kisses, thus throwing open the door unto enormous personal healing. The kiss of the mouth is the new paradigm manifested within the body of Christ.

Oh, please kiss me!

(See Proverbs 2:6–10; Psalm 85:10; Ephesians 4:13; John 3:29.)

"Oh let him kiss me with the kisses of the mouth" (1:2)

Your intimacy births genuine worship, as well as an interior personal knowledge of who you are. Let me hear you breathe.

How often I have said to a Bible class, pointing to the Scriptures, "This is not ink, but breath. This class is to move us into greater intimacy with the living God."

The poetry of The Song is not academically satisfying as are so many other books within the Bible. But in The Song God is seeking to romance the human heart. This is why He is now making this kissing relationship the issue. He is now offering us a radical, extravagant presence within our lives!

I have spent far more time on these words than on any of the other scriptures within The Song of Songs. The reason is because I have found too many church people who are profoundly offended over these words. But the offense truly is the result of the overall defilement within our culture, which we have absorbed day in and day out. Who of us have clean hearts in that we can truly respond to this word in purity?

We need to respect Him here. God doesn't seem to have any trouble saying, "Kiss me." But religious people don't say things like this about their god. It's because their gods are solid rock, or close to it.

He understands the enormous need we each have to personally experience His Bridegroom love. Why? Because we then grow in the knowledge of how close He is and how much He values the personal time we spend with Him. Within my heart and soul, kissing me is His extravagant glorious presence. Amen!

I have complained to God for over thirty years concerning the use of this phrase, "the kisses of the mouth." One day in the sanctuary of my church, He poured out His heart to me in that His people did not know Him. They were content to know *about* Him, but that was not enough. This scripture was coming from the outcry of the author's heart, directed to His people. Our relationship to the living God is far too religious and far too casual.

> *This profound merging into Your presence creates one who not only knows You and Your word, but it also births genuine worship within our tired, worn-out, unbelieving hearts.*
>
> *Worship merges us deeply within all that You are. Let the kissing begin! Be glorified, be beautifully known! Be deeply loved, be kissed again and again! You alone change my heart! Let Your glorious presence be extravagant within me!*

> Behold, I stand at the door and knock; if anyone hears
> My voice and opens the door.
> —REVELATION 3:20

He's not asking for this door to be opened so He can lecture us. The wonderful personal revelation is that He loves this time of intimacy within you and me. This revelation draws me in to say to Him, "Kiss me with the kisses of your mouth, for your love is sweeter than wine" (Song of Sol. 1:2).

(See John 4:23–24; Isaiah 61:10–11.)

"Oh let him kiss me with the kisses of his mouth" (1:2)

> Seek the LORD, and his strength; seek his face evermore.
> —PSALM 105:4

David, Solomon's father, wrote this psalm to be sung as God's people carried the ark of the covenant from the house of Obededom into Jerusalem.

"Let me see your face" is an established theme throughout the Psalms proclaiming heart hunger. Crying out for more, then more, and oh, so much more of His grace!

But the surprise in The Song is that this tenacious Lover of life is after our hearts! He is after a solid relationship within us. Not to condemn, but to love us as intimately as we allow Him to. When we regularly open the door to His knocking, He is not pressing into us simply to give us a message. He does not move closer to simply tell us something. In every way we will grow in discerning the depth of His presence. Not omnipresence, but deep personal presence!

I have personally experienced a deeper awareness of how close He lives to me and in me. There is a sweetness of the silence of His companionship within the depths of my being. What does He want me to experience and to know? Quiet intimacy, yes kissing intimacy of His powerful presence! He and His Son are essentially this message.

> *Life on earth assaults the human heart and shrinks it. But now it's about Your beautiful heart connecting more fully within mine. You come to me as the Lover of my soul. I don't need to deserve this, but simply to say yes to your kisses. This quality of revelation I hunger for.*

This relationship creates a marriage union.

Bernard of Clairveaux speaks of His kiss in this way:

> For the favor of the kiss bears with it a twofold gift, the light of knowledge and the fervor of devotion. He is in truth the Spirit of wisdom and insight, who, like the bee carrying its burden of wax and honey, is fully equipped with the power both of kindling the light of knowledge and infusing the delicious nurture of grace. Two kinds of people therefore may not consider themselves to have been gifted with the kiss. Those who know the truth without loving it, and those who love it without understanding it; from which we conclude that this kiss leaves room neither for ignorance nor for lukewarmness.[1]

(See Psalm 27:8–9; Colossians 2:2–5; 1 Corinthians 2.)

"Oh let him" (1:2)

This outcry of the heart is expressed by a woman's voice.

But God wrote The Song. Notice, she is saying, "Oh, let *him*," and not *you*, which signifies distance. He will do everything within our lives to close up this distance between us.

> *We have forgotten, Oh, Lord, that physical love woven into godly love all originates from Your heart. It is about Your love and I now return this unto You. Use this metaphor of the "kisses of the mouth" and Your closeness to me to open up a whole new relationship in You.*
>
> *What's it going to take to make my daily life more about the living God, and not always about me? So kiss me and fill my heart with Your grace! Lord, my heart cries out: no more casual encounters! Kiss me in intimate revelations of Your beauty and holiness. Allow intimacy in You to define who I am.*

(See John 1:14; Proverbs 2:6–7; 2 Chronicles 30:8–9.)

"Oh let him kiss me with the kisses of his mouth" (1:2)

Within our scriptures the journey of the Father's heart on earth is described:

> And I will dwell among the people of Israel, and will be their God and they shall know that I am the Lord.
>
> —Exodus 29:45

He creates the tabernacle system for this purpose. He completes His yearning when:

> The word became flesh and dwelt among us, full of grace and truth; we have beheld his glory, glory as of the only son of the Father.
>
> —John 1:14

And now He moves still closer.

> Behold I stand at the door and knock; if anyone hears my voice and opens the door, I will come into him and eat with him and he with me.
>
> —Revelation 3:20

In the progression of God's plan, His dwelling place has become increasingly more intimate. From afar He has come very close, breathing close; to enjoy us as His Son's bride. The wonderful truth is that He chose us long before it ever entered our minds to choose Him. His personal love for each of us has always been framed in intimacy. In Jesus' prayer for the church, He says,

> I have made known to them thy name, and I will make
> it known, that the love with which thou hast loved me
> may be in them, and I in them.
>
> —JOHN 17:26

> For God so loved the world that he gave…
>
> —JOHN 3:16

And He gave and gave and then gave still more! Within the drawing power of His love, He draws us closer and still closer and still more. His love calls for intimacy.

God has created the marriage relationship, or the kissing relationship, with those who will enter into His covenant love.

> *Kiss my heart and redirect my heart's energies. Kiss my
> eyes, my ears and my mouth, that I may speak words full
> of life within You.*

(See Psalm 73:28; Hebrews 7:23, 4:16, 7:19; John 6:44; John 17.)

"For your love is better than wine" (1:2)

My opinion is that she's been kissed. She now speaks to us using *"your"* and not *his*. How quickly He responds to her. Truthfully she probably was lost, but not *that* lost. If you too define yourself as lost, then know you are not hopelessly lost. His tenacious love is seeking you out now, and He knows where you are.

The wine of the fullness of God's Spirit flowing through the Bridegroom creates within us a heart which cannot get enough. We are desperate for His wine; but what is it? It's the fullness of His beautiful presence which is able to saturate us body, soul, and spirit. His kisses capture our hearts and souls. It is an intensely personal kiss which has a saturating quality. The empty heart which cried out is now being filled!

Wine speaks of a beautiful interior experience of the Holy Spirit. Within the inner man heart knowledge is far more encompassing. We experience within our soul and spirit the dynamic of His very presence and the power of His intensely loving heart. This dynamic may never be reduced to mere emotionalism, even if my personal response is shallow. He is deep and His embraces draw me into eternity.

> *Your love is sweeter than wine, and anything else I replace You with. You are more eternally real than all the stuff I choose over You. Reveal in me Your beauty, Your love, and Your presence. Teach me about You!*

> That the God of our Lord Jesus Christ, the Father of glory, may give you a spirit of wisdom and of revelation in the knowledge of him, having the eyes of your heart enlightened.
>
> —EPHESIANS 1:17–18

"For your love is better than wine" (1:2)

> *It was at the wedding feast in Cana where You first supplied the human heart with Your wine. Those who partook said it was the best wine. Your life, even then, was appointed to attend other wedding feasts when You became the Bridegroom of the human heart.*

And we, then, are His chosen bride. At this wedding Christ created and then served the best wine, which would begin to bind hearts internally with the Father's.

> *And You are choosing us potentially as Your bride? This takes our breath away because as yet, we haven't seriously chosen You!*

This marriage will connect us within His eternal flow of life.

And from his fullness have we all received grace upon
grace. For the law was given through Moses; grace and
truth came through Jesus Christ.

—John 1:16–17

Daily life flows through us night and day, leaving its debris. Everyday we need the blood of Christ to wash us clean. And every hour there is a life flow out of Him into me. This must be the wine house!

Sit in His presence, sit in His fullness. "Oh, heart and soul within me, be full and satisfied in His life flow; in His wine house!"

(See Ephesians 1:12; Luke 5:36–39; Psalm 104:14–15; Jeremiah 31:12.)

"Your anointing oils are fragrant" (1:3)

*Your person is perfumed with the precise fragrances which
draw the human heart to Yourself. You are the only one in
the universe who has given all to fully love us.*

Great truth, please engrave it within me!

*Nothing is lovely about any of us, and yet Your heart
is hungry to love us deeply. I am called to live out my life
in this personal knowledge, not only about me, but more
about You.*

We may have little understanding of the beautiful person we are approaching, but He fully knows us, and it's not a problem. How important it is we learn how to focus on Him? I believe the soul from the dark tents was created to teach us these mysteries.

Having the eyes of your hearts enlightened, that you may
know what is the hope to which He has called you.

—Ephesians 1:18

(See Psalm 45:8–9; Mark 14:3.)

"Your name is oil poured out" (1:3)

> *You are never offering us just a little bit. But as Your*
> *people, that's just about all we ever experience...just a*
> *little bit. Your name, Your presence, has everything to do*
> *with Your fullness. The presence of spiritual life flowing*
> *from Your side, then from Your glorious exaltation, is more*
> *than enough.*

She simply asks, and then receives. She asked for intimacy, and the release of His oil and wine flowed into her. There is great healing for the one who seeks through His overflow of oil and wine. All she did was ask! No holy performance was required!

His desire for us is more than enough. Our asking for His kiss of the mouth expands us body, soul, and spirit, for Him to lavish upon us all that He is prepared to give us. Her journey in Him will open the eyes of our hearts into this marvelous truth; breathing vibrant truth.

(See Colossians 2:9–10, 1:19–20; Ephesians 1:5, 3:19, 1:2–3; John 1:14; 2 Corinthians 1:20; Psalms 16:11, 36:7–8; Acts 9:17.)

"Your name is oil poured out; therefore the virgins do love you" (1:3)

A dynamic relationship is now being cultivated. Loving God was never intended to be cooked up within our own emotional resources. Loving God has everything to do with allowing His Holy Spirit free access within us, body, soul, and spirit.

I once said to Him, "I don't love you. Let me be honest and get this out into the open." He answered, "I know you don't. But one day you will." He understood that truly it is His wine, His oil, and His Holy Spirit which authenticates me into loving Him.

What do I bring to this relationship? One weary soul, so tired of cooking up spiritual pretense. It's over! It truly is about Him!

> My sole possession is your love; in earth beneath, or
> heaven above, I have no other store; and though with

fervent plea I pray, And beseech you day after day, I ask
for nothing more.

—Madame Jeanne-Marie Guyon, 1648–1717

(See John 1:14; Colossians 2:9–10; Ephesians 1:5, 3:19; Acts 9:17;
2 Corinthians 1:20; Psalms 16:11, 45:7; Isaiah 1:4.)

"Draw me away, let us run after you" (1:4, NIV)

A life flow of revelation coming forth from His throne will create
this desire within us. It creates running legs! She, again, is the initiator, but she, as most of us, has been running on empty.

She is now moving closer to Him while carrying some very dark
baggage. But she is moving towards Him. It was never His intention
to drag her off. Sometimes I wish it were, but that's not His style of
loving.

In the outcry of her heart she must release the brakes to activate
her running legs. Human brakes come in all sizes and shapes; such
as, anger towards God and family, intellectual commitment to false
beliefs about God (as well as about herself), an unforgiving heart—
the list is long. But the brakes are off! The soul from the dark tents
now says, "Draw me, and I will run after you!"

I love this scripture and the enormous release it performs within
me. How long He has waited to hear this from that very "me" who
causes "me" so many problems and had "me" running after worthless, damaging rendezvous.

> Draw near to God and he will draw near to you.
>
> —James 4:8

He needs to hear these words from us, "Kiss me and now draw
me!" He is never ambivalent concerning me. The lady from the dark
tents of life pursued His presence, not casually, nor once in awhile.
At the very beginning of this book she searched for intimacy.

(See Hebrews 4:26; 7:18, 25; 10:1, 22; 11:06; Psalm 119:2, 10.)

"The King has brought me into his chambers" (1:4, NIV)

How quickly He responds! The Father God continues to sing to us. The melody of His great love wafts over our walls of ignorance and spiritual blindness. This song He continually sings into the dark places of our souls—those precise places cultivating unbelief.

And at some point, in our own words, we say to Him, "Draw me after you!" He leaps into action bringing her into His chambers. He doesn't hesitate! He's waited a long, long time.

"Well, He's never done this for me." But how do you know? Perhaps you've been too busy and focused on too many other things; perhaps working too hard to please Him when He first desires to utterly please you.

She wants more of Him—music to His ears! But how can I believe all this? The soul from the dark tents is no prize. What in the world is He thinking? And besides, this is just poetry.

That's where I've always been wrong. Indeed, in His heart this soul is a trophy. Anyone at anytime who is hungering for more of Him is a potential diamond.

This scripture has always ministered deeply to my heart for it dispelled several false beliefs in my personal faith system. One, I truly must become one of His chosen few to grow spiritually, just like those in church who do everything right; who simply glow.

The second belief is I had to find the chambers on my own. I possess a wandering heart. I am unable on my own to ever find that door to glorious intimacy in Christ. It will never happen! I am simply not spiritual enough!

In Christ this precisely happens! He says,

> And I tell you, ask and it will be given you; seek and you will find; knock, and it will be opened to you.
> —Luke 11:9–10

> Thou dost make him glad with the joy of thy presence.
> —Psalm 21:6

She is teaching us these things. She asks, (Song of Sol. 1:2), she seeks, (v. 4), and she finds, (v. 7).

(See Psalms 9:10, 14:2, 22:26, 24:6–10, 34:10, 40:16, 53:2, 70:4, 105:3–4.)

"The king has brought me into His chambers" (1:4)

The speaker tells us that "the King has brought me into His chambers." He brought *me*! The big stubborn *me*, He brought into chamber revelation. His desire is that all His people would know His chamber quality of loving.

Chambers in the Hebrew language is "wine house." The Holy Spirit insists on using this controversial image. But I have come to understand that it defines His quality of knowledge birthed within us. After all, His kisses are sweeter than wine. The wine of heaven anoints us within all the joy of His loving presence—Father, Son, and Holy Spirit.

I know Him! In Scriptures, the living Word, I hear Him breathe! But you might respond saying, "How can this be?" It is possible to simply know something *about* Him and still not discern His personal presence within our lives.

This has everything to do with the outpouring of the Holy Spirit. He creates the truth of His presence authentically within us—nothing pretentious, only eternity. God seeks that we worship Him in Spirit and in truth. His fullness of life is both, overflowing wine.

> The drawing power of the person of the Lord Jesus
> Himself generates the pursuing power within us. If the
> Lord draws us by the revelation of Himself through His
> Spirit, then the seeking after Him is relatively easy.
> —WATCHMAN NEE[2]

Draw me now and fill me with the wine of Your presence.
Fill me with this quality of personal knowledge in You.
Draw me after You, and I will come.

(See Psalm 27:4; John 14:22–23.)

"Into his chambers" (1:4)

In His chambers the cleansing of the leper begins. In His chambers the healing and restoration begins; immersed into the most loving relationship that exists. The heart who is saying, "Draw me and I will come," is a troubled heart, a product of the dark fields of life. Darkness of heart and soul are the natural products of her family line.

She somehow focused on the Bridegroom of the heart and cried out, "Kiss me!" And then, "Draw me after You and I will run!" That was enough for Him to hear. This heart does not need to prove itself.

Because we are essentially lame and blind and definitely hard of hearing in our relationship with the living God, I believe He picked her up and carried her into His chambers. It is never completely left up to us to maintain and complete our journey of faith in Him.

In Revelation 3:20 God's Word tells us that He stands at the door and knocks waiting for us to open that door. This concerns heart intimacy. He has chosen us for intimacy in His presence. His magnificent heart longs to merge within the heart of the door opener, and that's about all I am capable of doing. I can open this door within me and invite intimacy with the living God.

This requires our time. How special is His sublime presence as He changes our hearts, opens our eyes, and ultimately changes the makeup of who we are. He's not there to give us a message, for He's the message. He's there to love on the interior heart.

We are to know Him as the Lover of our souls. He is never religious dogma.

The chambers are not the bedroom. But they are a place to draw close to Him. It truly is within His presence our lives change. He's never dogma, He's vibrant breathe!

Oh, such a heart we approach! This journey in The Song will connect your heart more fully to His. Let His passions flow!

> *Take me away with You! Let us hurry! Let the King bring me into His chambers.*

"We will exult and rejoice in you" (1:4)

The spectators in The Song are defined in a number of ways; as the chorus, the virgins, and the daughters of Jerusalem. They now speak. They have never experienced what is going on within her, but they observe life fullness. They do not see the King, but a desire for Him is being birthed within them. So they follow her around. He is wonderfully contagious.

It is unclear, however, whether they are saying this about the King, or about her. I suspect it's about her.

"We will extol your love more than wine" (1:4)

Now the chorus is repeating her words of worship in 1:2. She shared her testimony of kissing closeness. She's also telling them of His quick response to the outcries of her heart. He was never apathetic about her.

She is created to teach us as well about this journey of the heart into His fullness. She is God's instrument to reach our hearts and tell us that each of us has an appointed intimacy in Him. Apathy creates distance and this distance originates within us.

(See Colossians 1:27–29.)

"Rightly do they love you" (1:4)

The chorus is still speaking. Obviously some dramatic changes are seen in her, and they sense it has everything to do with Him. The daughters of Jerusalem are experiencing a life flow by hanging out with her. I suspect the fragrance of His person is evident. She really hasn't done much to create this. She never got her act together. She has simply pursued Him. It is enough!

She says, "Draw me and I'll run after you." Now they may be saying, "Draw us closer that we might do the same."

"I am dark, but lovely, O daughters of Jerusalem, like the tents of Kedar, like the curtains of Solomon" (1:5, NIV)

Much praise and adoration is being directed to her. But she now sets these ladies straight. "Don't stare at me! Don't examine me! I am one dark lady from the dark tents of Kedar. These are my natural roots and they define who I am."

Psalm 120 may be the shortest and the strangest of all of the Psalms. The psalmist cries out,

> In my distress I cried unto the Lord and he heard me.
> —PSALM 120:1

He then ends his prayer in this way:

> I have dwelt too long with one who hates peace. I am for
> peace; but when I speak; they are for war.
> —PSALM 120:6–7

"Oh, please get me out of this place! I can't stand it any longer!"

Where was this awful place and who were these terrible people? The tents of Kedar, our lady's natural roots. Their premise for living is in total opposition to everything the King stands for. Being lost and unlovely is a terrible condition to find yourself in. But in the next few scriptures she will precisely describe herself as just that.

Our lady cried out to the King for a change of address. When we push into Him our hearts mean business. We want radical change, and we want this King to be the center of it.

(See John 14:6; Psalm 120.)

"But lovely like the curtains of Solomon" (1:5)

The King brought her into His chambers for many reasons. First it is to spend time with Him and allow the fullness of His life flow to impact all that she is. Second, to see her destiny in Him unfold.

He has such a marvelous vision custom made for each one of us. These are His same desires for us: to first spend time with Him, and second to grow, then grow some more and still more in His presence within us.

At present, her knowledge of herself is a dark knowledge. Dark places create darkness in the heart and the soul. Ultimately it births within us such a distorted picture as to whom we are. As she is teaching us about herself, she then reveals who we are.

Our high priest in the Book of Hebrews in the New Testament teaches us to draw near in Him as He moves God's people into the Holy of Holies.

> Therefore brethren, since we have confidence to enter the sanctuary by the blood of Jesus, by a new and living way which he has opened for us through the curtain which is his flesh, and since we have a great priest over the house of God, let us draw near with a true heart in full assurance of faith.
>
> —Hebrews 10:19–22

King Solomon was appointed by God to build the first permanent temple in Jerusalem for God's presence to abide. Solomon's curtains were throughout this beautiful tabernacle. They were appropriately woven in the finest of linen to glorify the presence of the living God. The same heavenly designs of the images of the high places are now being woven within in the substance of who she is. She is destined for the high places, where He reigns and His glory abounds. His presence weaves His glory within us.

She is a duality. She is still connected to her natural roots, but she is also experiencing chamber love that authenticates her by the weaving of His life force within her. In His presence glory happens!

Teach us your ways. They draw us far beyond our natural selves.

(See 1 Corinthians 12–13; Ephesians 1:3–10; Isaiah 62:3–5, 61:3–4; Colossians 1:9–14; 1 Chronicles 29:10–13.)

"Do not gaze at me because I am swarthy, because the sun has scorched me" (1:6)

"You don't really know me yet. The natural image of God in me is so damaged, I hardly know who I am. Don't stare at me! Don't examine me!"

The word *sun* is a metaphor of the ruling principle within this soul's life. It is sin—hers, as well as the sins of others.

"I am dark," she is saying, the meaning of *swarthy*. This soul is saying, "I am stained. I am damaged goods. Don't examine me too closely. Keep your distance."

(See Ephesians 1:3–10; Proverbs 23:7.)

"My mother's sons were angry with me, they made me keeper of the vineyards" (1:6)

In the Middle East a beautiful daughter would never be forced to be a field laborer. Her skin would be scorched and her worth to the family would be ruined. No, this daughter, because of her natural beauty, would be pampered.

She would be married off to a wealthy older man and the family's net worth and influence would be greatly enhanced. Many times the beautiful daughter was used for this purpose and this was not necessarily a great personal blessing to her.

The other daughter was put out into the field as forced labor. She was not valued by the heads of her family. They saw no worth in her. Who would ever desire her in marriage? Her mother's sons were angry with her. She was no trophy. She did not please anyone.

(Philippians 1:6, 3:14, 20, 21.)

"But my own vineyard I have not kept" (1:5)

God never destined this soul to live out her life drowning in sin—hers as well as the family's. He hangs around all those who are slaves in the fields of life, and He waits for the outcry of the human heart.

She finally focused on Him and said, "Kiss me with the kisses of your mouth. Love me intimately, for no one else does."

How presumptuous! How could He ever see anything of value within her? How can one so desirable love someone so undesirable?

It is not His passion to see her submerged into guilt. Neither is it His desire to see her lost in the personal damage she has experience within her family line. Is this life truly worth saving?

The Song of Songs has been written to be sung into hearts precisely like hers, fully damaged. It is to draw us into Him. He has so much to personally offer to each one of us.

"Oh, heart of mine, listen to the beautiful music of His heart. Oh, listen… He sings to me. Seek His face, He is waiting." Is it getting too mushy? I surely hope so.

> The Lord is good to those who wait for him, to the soul
> that seeks him. It is good that one should wait quietly
> for the salvation of the Lord.
>
> —Lamentations 3:25–26

(See Matthew 11:28; John 4:10; Isaiah 21:16; Lamentations 3:57–66; Psalm 25:7.)

"Tell me, you whom my soul loves" (1:7)

"Tell me!" He is personable and close to me throughout my day. He is fully able to "tell me." He is fully able to love me intimately. He already has. Her request, "tell me," is not a problem for Him. He's been waiting to do this for most of her life.

The Word in The Song is a person, not simply a theology. The Truth is after our hearts! His kisses create heart knowledge. He is a transforming truth! He is not simply trying to educate her. He's out to win the bride within her. He wants a kissing relationship with this one. His words are Spirit and life. In speaking to Him she experiences His life flow within her.

> I am the way, and the truth, and the life; no one comes
> to the Father but by me.
>
> —John 14:6

His kiss, His wine, His oil, His beauty, His presence draws this dark soul fervently to Himself! The concession of her heart has been radically changed. It is no longer about her past and the anger she endured. She now focuses on Him and her life is profoundly being turned inside out. "Kiss me, draw me, and now tell me!" are the outcries of her heart.

God created this guide to teach each of us about the journey of the heart and soul. These outcries teach us to pursue Him, no matter who we are and where we come from. And it does not matter how much dark baggage we drag along with us. He knows all of this. Thus, little by little, that stuff we travel with will drop off…in His presence. We have allowed all that stuff to define who we are, and it isn't at all "who we are." This sweet truth is a kiss.

"Kiss me with the kisses of your mouth for your love is sweeter than wine" (1:2).

"Just set that ugly baggage down." But perhaps she is unable to. Through dark circumstances it has become embedded in her and perhaps within us as well. It powerfully defines who we now are. But His wine has a saturating effect. It is full of His glory!

But now she is in the presence of a powerful flow of life. He fully accepts her, and all that stuff will automatically begin to drop off. It was never up to her to clean up her act. She did the right thing in seeking intimacy with Him. His person, His presence is capable of changing everything! His life flow is heaven's wine.

We may call out to Him using different words, such as, deliver me, give me a job, heal my body, and so on. He does honor our asking for these things, but there must come a time when the outcries are for Him alone.

This road into intimacy has been created for each of us, not simply for the beautiful spiritual people. Where are you? In prison? Nothing can lock out His pursuing love from a heart searching for Him. Nothing!

Love me just as I am, and I will become someone I never knew existed.

> Blessed is he whom thou dost choose and bring near, to
> dwell in thy courts. We shall be satisfied with the good-
> ness of thy house, thy holy temple.
>
> —PSALM 65:4

(See Matthew 22:7; Jeremiah 29:10–14; Psalm 86:11; John 14:1; Luke 12:31–34.)

"Where you pasture your flock, where you make it lie down at noon" (1:7)

It's now time to establish new priorities as to whom she will hang out with. Who will now have the greatest influence in her life? "Make it lie down" means all of this.

The metaphor *noon*, describes a greater and more complete revelation of Him. Noon is the fullness of light. This third outcry is directing her into a greater commitment of time well spent with Him.

> Make me to know thy ways, O Lord; teach me thy paths,
> lead me in thy truth, and teach me, for thou art the God
> of my salvation; for thee I wait all the day long.
>
> —PSALM 25:4–5

She asked for running legs and she ran. Now she wants more, which requires sitting still and silencing her inner noise. She now asks for a heart at rest and fully satisfied in His presence. Her journey has just begun by sitting quietly.

This personal knowledge birthed within each of us as to sitting and resting is one of the strongest themes in The Song. A stranger to the faith in Christ may ask us, "How do you know Him so well?" We sit quietly in His presence. There is a fullness of life within Him and He overflows within me.

> For we are strangers before thee, and sojourners, as all
> our fathers were, our days on earth are like a shadow,
> and there is no abiding.
>
> —1 CHRONICLES 29:15

(See Isaiah 40:30–31; 1 Corinthians 2:9; 1 Kings 2:1–4; Psalm 17:15.)

"For why should I be like one who wanders beside the flocks of your companions?" (1:7)

In Hebrew the word *wanders* also means "one who is veiled." The thought of being veiled could produce a wandering heart.

This scripture blesses my heart in that He is not afraid to draw me just as I am. I can trust in His presence to know which way to proceed. Where will she go from here? What is she to do? These are not the most important questions. We all live veiled in the poverty of our knowledge of the living God.

After dark, while living in Iran, I would leave my house to walk down an alleyway to the main street. It was there I could buy milk. How often I would see a black clump as in a pile of black cloth. As I drew closer an elderly hand would reach out begging for money. This woman was covered in poverty and darkness of soul.

I always tried to have something to give because I did not know what harsh circumstances covered her life. The air was cold and the night was dark, not at all pleasant circumstances. Perhaps she was forced out into the cold and could not return home until she brought back some contribution to the family. Possibly she was simply veiled in poverty where there was no place to return to.

Many of those things which veil us create a murky interior life, which was never God's plan for us. We store up unhappy memories, tragedies, losses, failures, etc. They all cause us to wander spiritually, emotionally, and perhaps, even physically.

> *Tell me, You whom my soul loves. Redirect my wandering heart to time well spent in your presence.*

He can't resist this. He has given too much to establish intimacy within our hearts, no matter what condition He finds them in.

> As for me, I shall behold thy face in righteousness; when
> I awake, I shall be satisfied with beholding thy form.
>
> —Psalm 17:15

"If you do not know" (1:8)

"Oh, Lord, don't you understand this woman who is coming to you? This woman from the dark tents is damaged goods." By her own words she says, "The sun has scorched me. I have not kept my own vineyards. "

"And yet you search the earth precisely for hearts like hers." He greets her with a huge smile. "Not a problem," He answers. "She wants more of Me. She cried out to Me, 'Give me running legs and I will come to You.'

"She is welcomed into My presence. I have waited for this one from the dark tents for a long, long time. And now she comes." (The flow of His heart into mine.)

(See Revelation 22:17; Psalm 116:7; Matthew 11:28–29; 1 Chronicles 16:29.)

"Most beautiful among women" (1:8)

My first response was negative to His greeting in scripture. I never liked flirting.

"Lord, this is insulting. How could this ever be said of this person? Let's be honest. Who are you kidding?"

He answered me, "I will never interpret or define who you are based on the foundation of your brokenness. In Me this is truly not who you are destined to become. You are chosen to reflect who I am in this broken world. I have poured out My heart and life to create in you My beauty. Authentically moving towards Me will make you genuinely beautiful and filled with My glory."

My entire destiny changed in this precious conversation. Now who do I chose to believe?

"Heart of mine, become discerning as to whom you will choose to listen."

Oh, please, create within me a listening believing heart.

Study the Psalms, which are personal prayers found in the very center of our Scriptures. Often they begin with the outcries of the psalmist's heart. But if you notice some way through the prayer, the voice changes and it is God's heart speaking. They become personal conversations.

How much God longs to establish within each of us a listening heart. He has great things to say to us. But His desire has never been that we simply know something about Him. His desire is that we know Him as deeply and as intimately as possible, no matter where we now find ourselves.

(See Revelation 3:20–21; Jeremiah 31:3–4; Psalm 81:5–16.)

"Most beautiful" (1:8)

Words connect and sometimes bind us to a spirit. His words connect us to the fullness of the heart of God. His words are Spirit and life. His words draw us into holy communion with the living God. Does this change us? Yes, it makes us beautiful.

True beauty flows from the heart of God. His beauty is merged into His glorious presence. We hang out with Him, and we too merge into authentic beauty.

> One thing have I asked of the Lord, that will I seek after; that I may dwell in the house of the Lord all the days of my life, to behold the beauty of the Lord, and to inquire in his temple.
>
> —PSALM 27:4

(See Psalms 50:1–2, 130:5; Acts 7:20.)

"I compare you, my love" (1:9)

Throughout The Song He will address her as "my love." This king has the heart of a lover. He insists on being very personal. She cried out for intimacy precisely with Him, and that she will experience.

How close? Is it really possible to be intimate with Him, the Savior of the world? She will now answer Him as "my beloved." This will help the reader of The Song to understand who is speaking. The Song will show us the quality of intimacy we are freely able to experience "in Him."

However, in The Song there are times we don't know who is

speaking. But it doesn't matter because this message is flowing out of the heart of the Father God. It flows from His passion, who asked His Son to first become our Savior and then our glorious Lord and then within us, the intimate Bridegroom of our hearts.

> *Open the ears of our hearts, Lord, so that we do not journey through life without ever hearing these sweet words from You. Oh, please help us not to choose to live in total ignorance through the misguidance of our souls.*

He says, "Get intimate with Me. I hunger for your presence, now hunger for Mine."
(See Ephesians 1:5–23.

"I compare you, my love" (1:9)

Do we at all comprehend what is birthed within us when we choose to spend time in His presence? What happens within me? I become beautiful! His presence, His person, first transforms the heart. Then, little by little, works on the rest of me. It's His time table, not mine. He simply loves being with me.

> Christ in you, the hope of glory.
>
> —Colossians 1:27

> May mercy, peace, and love be multiplied to you.
>
> —Jude 1:2

May mercy, peace and love be lavished upon you!
(See Colossian's 1:21–29; Psalm 32:10.

"I compare you, my love, to a mare of Pharaoh's chariots" (1:9)

King Solomon received all of his glory and riches from the living God.

> Behold I give you a wise and discerning mind, so that none like you has been before you and none like you shall arise after you. I give you also what you have not

asked, both riches and honor, so that no other king shall
compare with you, all your days.

—1 Kings 3:12–13

What would be the most appropriate vehicle for the appearance
in public of a glorious king? A Rolls Royce, of course. In Solomon's
day there were the magnificently beautiful horses from Egypt. He
owned stables full of them, and I am sure they received the best of
care.

If he wore beautiful robes and a spectacular head covering of
brocade, feathers, and jewels, then it is likely his horse displayed
similar adornment reflecting Solomon's kingly status.

He defines who she now is, as one most appropriate to reveal
the presence of this glorious King to her world. She seemed to be
the one who first chose Him. But the scriptures teach us that He
destined us in love.

He chose me long before any longing for Him existed within me.
He first chose me. He chose me to bear His glory.

(See Ephesians 1:4–5, 3:17, 5:2; 1 John 4:16; 2 Timothy 1:3.)

"Your cheeks are comely with ornaments, your neck with strings of jewels" (1:10)

He now lavishes His glory and His beauty on the one who will
spend time in His presence. God saturated the earth with His Son's
blood to completely save us. Every drop of water and blood poured
out of God's Lamb to draw us as close as possible to Himself.

Time in His presence has a demanding effect within us, body,
soul, and spirit. I wonder if it is at all possible to spend any time
with Him and not be changed, to some extent, by His glory. Is it
possible? Allow my personal faith to grow in His direction.

He now lavishes her with jewels; gold and silver and precious
gems. The Bible uses the metaphor of gems to somehow describe
to us His enormous eternal beauty. This lifts us out of the realm of
natural beauty.

But how in the world does she deserve this? He has never said,
"Get yourself cleaned up." When we go to church we normally clean

up to create the proper appearance. Usually it is this that we focus on; the proper outward appearance.

The Song shows me that it is essentially about Him; pursuing Him and allowing His beauty, His life to saturate who I am. It is about Him, but in union with Him it becomes also about me. He changes me body, soul, and spirit. But the choice is essentially mine.

> And we all with unveiled face, beholding the glory of the Lord are being changed into his likeness from one degree of glory to another; for this comes from the Lord who is the Spirit.
>
> —2 CORINTHIANS 3:18

Her heart cried out for face-to-face intimacy, for His chambers and His glory and wow! He now lavishes her with jewels! As her heart is changing she more and more wears His incomparable beauty. This transforming power now embracing her is more about His presence, not His mandates.

(See Ephesians 2:10, 3:19–20; 1 Peter 1:3–7; 2 Corinthians 4:17; Colossians 1:27.)

"We will make you ornaments of gold, studded with silver" (1:11)

It is always about Him, His beautiful presence. It's not so much about my feelings from my past or who I am now or in my future. His fullness brings us into every spiritual blessing in the high places. He not only captivates our interior person but there He will dwell in intimacy. And that all began with His kisses which represented His radical presence!

His love is transforming love. That which heaven requires of us will be authentically birthed or created within us. Our hearts are drawn to Him, as truly the Lover of our souls.

The great secret, now made fully known, is that we are changed in His glorious presence!

How it continually amazes me that she, as a lady from the dark tents, is greeted with such love! He lavishes His beauty within her as one He values and treasures. No junk jewelry will ever be worn by her; only the real stuff which is the quality of His workmanship, as well as His glory.

Silver represents redeemed humanity and gold His divinity and glory. The two now come together in His presence. In intimacy His glory is naturally, supernaturally birthed within her. She will now naturally, supernaturally glorify Him within her person.

(See 1 Chronicles 16:29; Psalms 27:4, 45:10–11; Isaiah 43:7, 61:2; Ephesians 2:8–10; Proverbs 3:13–15.)

"While the King was on his couch, my nard gave forth its fragrance" (1:12)

The one crying out is now silent. She is genuinely focused. The dark roots, which strangled any joy or knowledge that she would ever experience authentic love, are shrinking and disappearing. At present she has few words to describe to us what is happening. There are no concepts, simply the birthing of a deep personal knowledge and inner beauty. The value of spikenard is in its roots, and by spending time in Him her roots are sinking into His authentic life flow.

What is really going on? His transforming love! We are objects of a world which has transformed us, and consequently we then become its victims. What we have lost sight of is that He changes the fiber of our beings. But first His roots of divine life are changing the very substance of who she is. Transforming love is in His presence!

> Abide in me, and I with you.
>
> —JOHN 15:4

He says there is mutuality here. This relationship was never designed to be a one-sided conversation. It was never designed in that she simply appears before Him to get her daily orders. He now comes to her full of grace and truth, (John 1:14), as He does to us.

"My nard gave forth its fragrance" (1:12)

She focused on Him in the outcries of her heart. Now He focuses on her. He now has her. So preach to her! Get all that stuff in her straightened out! You have her attention, so give her the program! Get her going! There is so much to get done. Do it! And He does not. No program, simply more of Himself; simply more of His presence.

Something far greater is happening. In His presence internal as well as eternal changes are taking place. Her nard breaks forth, the deep roots of her heart are changing. She is exchanging the ties to the dark tents with sweet ties in Him. Focused worship does this. Hudson Taylor expresses it this way:

> It is His presence and through His grace that whatever of fragrance or beauty which may be found in us, comes forth. Of Him as its source, through Him as its instrument, and to Him as its end, is all that is gracious and divine. But *He himself* is better by far, than all that His grace works within us.[4]

The Father understands all of this. The Holy Spirit understands this and promotes full worship to take place within our hearts.

> *Lord, help me now to discern what I am worshiping day in and day out. It's those things I cannot live without. May the life roots of my heart break open and be an expansion of who You are in my life. May the depth of my heart know You intimately.*

His love, His abiding presence, is the dynamic which makes us fully beautiful.

(See Matthew 11:28; Psalms 23:2–3, 45:8–9; 1 Thessalonians 5:23–24; 1 Samuel 12:20–22.)

"My beloved is to me a bag of myrrh" (1:13)

> It was a pleasant thing to be in a chamber perfumed with myrrh. Through the nostrils myrrh conveys delight to

the human mind, but Christ gives delight to his people,
not through one channel, but through every avenue.[5]
—CHARLES SPURGEON[4]

In every way myrrh is a rich substance, not only as a fragrance but as that which forms the base for the world's most expensive perfumes.

Myrrh has preserving qualities as it was used to embalm. Within us myrrh preserves God's image. Not as a substance apart from His presence, but as a fragrance pouring forth from the holy of holies. He is fully desirable to the human heart who worships Him. Myrrh has enormous drawing power as well as binding power unto Him.

Myrrh is also used as a means of healing. Jehovah Rophi: "I am the Lord that healeth thee" (Exod. 15:26). He is full of new life in that He restores as well as heals.

His presence pours over her, setting her free to make internal choices to pursue Him. "Wake up my heart and learn from her. She is teaching you about yourself and this sublime journey of the heart." What I personally lack He produces within me.

(See Exodus 30:22, 33; Matthew 2:11; John 19:39; Psalm 45:8.)

"...that lies between my breasts" (1:13)

Who controls her world and her guilt over unproductive vineyards, as well as her anger with her brothers? Or is it the one who seeks His kisses and will run after Him. Is it the one who sits and worships His dynamic presence? The Song was written to birth these same desires within us.

This bag of myrrh, which represents His presence within her, now covers her heart and establishes her love life. It also enhances her quality of life whether in Him or within the world. His fragrance is the dynamic saturating power of the Holy Spirit within her.

Myrrh was an important ingredient in the holy anointing oil used only within the holy place, as well as the holy of holies. It filled these places with a beautiful fragrance drawing us to the living God. When the priests left this area, they naturally wore this same wonderful fragrance on their person.

> You love righteousness and hate wickedness. Therefore
> God, your God, has anointed you with the oil of glad-
> ness above your fellows; your robes are all fragrant with
> myrrh and aloes and cassia.
>
> —Psalm 45:7–8

"My beloved is to me a cluster of henna blossoms in the vineyard of Engedi" (1:14)

Scripture says to be filled with the Holy Spirit, which is His dynamic power and presence within us today. The vineyard of Engedi
is a metaphor of this fullness. She is using this thought to describe
to us His allure. His fullness changes who we are. I believe Solomon understood this as He grew up in the presence of the Lord in
David's tabernacle. It is interesting that God tells us that it is this
tabernacle which He loves to spend time in.

> After this, I will return, and I will rebuild the dwelling
> of David, which has fallen; I will rebuild its ruins, and
> I will set it up, that the rest of men may seek the Lord,
> and the gentiles who are called by my name, says the
> Lord, who has made these things known of old.
>
> —Acts 15:16–18

Solomon created and owned the vineyards at Engedi, which were
renowned throughout his world for the quality and quantity of its
harvest.

Henna has the meaning of ransom price. It also stains a deep red,
as the fullness of the blood of Christ stains us body, soul, and spirit.
Deep is the work of His presence as she soaks in Him. His blood-red
stain performs miraculous healing. Her relationship in Him is no
longer casual, but involved with His living fullness and excellence.

It is impossible to spend this quality time in Him and not be
authentically changed from within. Truth is taking up residence
within this one from the dark tents and creating within her an authentic new life. This song desires to birth within us glorious internal

knowledge of all that He is as Lover of our heart and soul; similar to a holy stain.

She's just beginning to understand these things. But what is taking place within her transcends human understanding. It's more about an authentic weaving of His divine qualities within her. Who owns these qualities? The Bridegroom of the human heart as well as all of us who pursue Him. The beauty of His life substance woven within us makes us authentic. She's not just a pretty face. No, His glory stains her inside out.

(See Acts 2:4, 9:17; Romans 15:14; Ephesians 5:18; Colossians 1:9; Luke 1:15, 41, 69; John 14:6.)

"Behold you are beautiful, my love; behold you are beautiful; your eyes are doves" (1:15)

He greets her with great affirmation. His first words, "Oh, you are beautiful," are repeated again for our benefit. The spirit of His words is full to overflowing with His delight.

"Oh, heart of mine, receive His word. For this is scripture written by the Holy Spirit to win my heart and soul to Him."

Dove's eyes are focused eyes. Doves are not equipped with lenses to see the entire vista of a landscape. They are not equipped to see the whole picture of life. But they are able to focus fully on Him. They see Him clearly. He fills the picture so it is all about Him.

Her eyes became increasingly focused as she cried out to Him for His kiss, His chambers, and a fullness of revelation as to who He is within her. She did not attain this on her own as in taking focus workshops. No, she simply pursued His presence.

Dove's eyes equip the heart to see in the power of the Holy Spirit. Dove's eyes reveal within us revelation flowing from God's throne. Her eyes are anointed with the ability and strength of eternal focus.

(See Matthew 3:16, 11:27–30).

"Behold, you are beautiful; your eyes are doves" (1:15)

I fought fear that even a personal Savior could never truly love me. Those who made up my root life never saw any genuine beauty in me. I was trash to them.

In complete embarrassment I could never present my face to this king. It's dirty, deformed. There is nothing lovely about me. Face-to-face means he'll look too closely and to deeply within me. An examination I cannot bear. Intimacy requires this.

This love song is written by the heart of an intensely loving God to capture our hearts. They may now be captured within the bars of a state.

But He's not fooling around! He does not run hot, then cold, especially towards her. His intentions are to draw us, just as we are, into a face-to-face relationship in Him; face-to-face and kissing close, no matter where we now live.

He will conquer self-hatred. His love transforms in every possible way. Where self-love is absent, He creates it, embodied within His power to love and to heal. He conquers everything which has conquered us. He equips us with dove's eyes, as most beautiful among women.

(See Ephesians 1:17–18.).

"Behold you are beautiful, my love" (1:15)

He calls her "My love." There is so much healing in these words spoken into a wounded heart. This song is reaching out in us through His same words: "My love." This word is full of His flowing life and glory—all which is appointed unto you and me. He says to us now, "My love." Now let us allow this life force to capture our hearts.

> *Jesus, our hearts have never heard this from You. Heal our inner wounds and draw us even more deeply into Your saving grace and life flow. Lord, we need to know You more intimately. You are not only a lion, fierce; but you're also a tender lover sent from the Father's heart to heal and to redeem our hearts and to make us yours.*

(See Psalms 27, 17:15.)

"Behold, you are beautiful, my beloved; truly lovely" (1:16)

Her response of faith repeats what He said to her. She naturally reflects His beauty. This is the result of the company she's keeping which is not at all casual but has become deeply personal.

This is a truth of life. We will reflect the dynamics of the strong elements within our lives; those things which drive us. In Christ we reflect His fullness! Wow! His beautiful fullness overflows and affects all that we are in Him. My confession of faith is to reflect my personal relationship in Him.

(See Colossians 1:19–20, 2:9–10; Ephesians 3:19, 1:2–3; 1 Corinthians 1:20; John 1:14; Psalms 16:11, 36:7–8; Acts 9:17.)

"Our couch is green" (1:16)

> I came that they may have life, and have it abundantly.
>
> —John 10:10

A personal relationship with this King was never designed to produce meagerness, inadequacy, or deficiency. God and His Son gave all to bring us into Bridegroom love. Their hearts overflow towards us, in that they may overflow within us.

Within the context of chamber love there is no manifestation of toil or drudgery. There should have been because this lady, fresh out of the dark tents, had so many unresolved problems. But look again! There is rest and enjoyment in His presence, and then more rest. Because the voice of our King said,

> It is done, complete, finished.
>
> —John 19:30

What's He doing? Basically nothing. He is not desperately trying to save her or keep her on the journey. How often I have seen my relationship in Christ precisely in these terms. As if He's always wringing His hands over me: "Now what are we going to do? She's always moving from crisis to crisis. She's one big problem!"

No, He has never confessed this over my life. And I am not to do it either! I am to honor and receive all that He births within me. This forms my personal confession of faith in Him.

New birth in Christ creates in us the authenticity of His beauty. Gold and silver bestows His glory. Roots established through His perfect relationship in the Father. He said,

> Lo I have come to do thy will. O God.
> —HEBREWS 10:7–10

I am to receive these gifts from Him and through Him. I am to focus and grow into all that He gives to me, revelation upon revelation.

His green couch speaks of rest, fullness, His presence, and more trusting rest in His beauty, in His power of obedience, in His knowledge of the living God, in His strength, in His life flow, then more and more and more. This couch is green, and this couch is appointed to provide a full rest in the heart and soul.

> I sought the Lord and he answered me, and delivered me
> from all my fears. Look to him and be radiant; so your
> face shall never be ashamed.
> —PSALM 34:4–5

(See Romans 5:15–16; Psalms 116:7, 132:14, 105:4–5; Jeremiah 6:16; Matthew 11:28–29; Hebrews 2:5, 10:7, 2 Thessalonians 1:5–7, Colossians 1:26–27.)

"The beams of our house are cedar, and our rafters are fir" (1:17)

Solomon's house was called the forest of Lebanon. He chose to build it with choice wood, impervious to decay. His heavenly Father is doing the same.

Sin destroys families. Sin is able to destroy every relationship on earth. The sin from the dark tents destroyed much within her.

When those closest to you see nothing good in you, then this is solid destruction.

The structure of her relationship with the King cannot be destroyed by sin. Sin within her heart is able to blind her faith, but the relationship still stands.

What He has accomplished for us is tied to eternity. His calling to love us is impervious to decay.

A feeling which has plagued me was: could I be sure His love for me would not grow cold as it did in other relationships? Would He not find me so imperfect, too weak, too defiled, too agitating that He would throw in the towel and withdraw His presence from me?

I don't deserve anything from Him. But this is a false premise to focus on. He chose me, and not at all based on anything lovely within me. The substance of His love for me, in me, about me, is the substance of His Father's covenant love, who says,

> I will never fail you nor forsake you.
> —HEBREWS 13:5

Heart of mine, please learn, that He loves me just as I am. He receives me, just as I am. We learn this from heaven's love song sung within us. Be filled with His music.

(See Hebrews 13:6–7, 13:21; Psalms 23, 100:5, 103:17; Isaiah 35:10, 54:8.)

"I am a rose of Sharon, a lily of the valley" (2:1)

The rose of Sharon is a common field flower. She is not a cultivated Perkin's rose. She is telling us that she is a very common person. Her birth, her blooming, her existence is incidental. She's no one special. Her personal bloom is seen for a very short season. Then it is gone!

Is she telling Him this or is she saying this for our benefit? I suspect it is for us.

"As a lily among brambles, so is my love among maidens" (2:2)

He corrects her. She truly is a lily and He loves spending time with her. The lily will be mentioned several times in The Song. But He does point out that although she is His lily, she is living out her earthly life in a real thorn patch in this world.

He calls her "My love," and for her He wore a crown of thorns. He knows her roots, and it was never a problem for Him. His crown of thorns on His head was her fallen life. He wore her thorns on His cross. It is finished! There is no problem here.

(See Mathew 7:15–16, 13:3–9, 27:29; Hebrews 6.

"As an apple tree among the trees of the wood" (2:3)

She is quick to reverse the comparison. She turns the spotlight back on him. He is not a common man. He is worth every minute, hour, and year we commit in spending time with Him.

If we lack authentic sweetness, she says we'll find it in Him. She has so much to teach us.

(See Psalm 21:6.)

"With great delight I sat in His shadow, and His fruit was sweet to my taste" (2:3)

"I sat. I chose to spend time with one who nurtured me in the fullness of life. Oh, it was good and so special!" she tells us.

Nothing else in life compares to His presence. Time in the Scriptures and time in praise unto worship creates within us an eternal beauty which reflects Him. She does not have to put on being spiritual. She simply spends time with Him. There is no sense of toil here or pressure, simply pure enjoyment!

(See Psalms 16:11, 51:11, 105:4, 119:9–10, 103; Proverbs 24:13–14; Luke 1:53.)

"He brought me to the banqueting house" (2:4)

> Blessed is he whom thou dost choose and bring near, to
> dwell in thy courts. We shall be satisfied with the good-
> ness of thy house, thy holy temple.
>
> —Psalm 65:4

The theme of The Song is to draw near. What was no relationship is now evolving into something wonderful within His life flow.
She's just beginning to enjoy the wealth of not only His house, but
more the wealth of His heart. The one traveling out of the darkness
of bankrupt hearts is now experiencing His divine fullness.

> Thou dost show me the path of life; in thy presence
> there is fullness of joy, in thy right hand are pleasures
> for evermore.
>
> —Psalm 16:11

"And his banner over me was love" (2:4)

I suspect, as with most hearts, our hunger for love and romance
caused us to make some bad personal choices. We were destined to
experience the deepest love possible. But, in heart hunger we drifted
into some painful relationships.

She now sits covered in authentic love, which she has never before experienced. This love is described as banners, and His name is
Jehovah Nissi.

In a war zone as avenging armies lined up for the conflict, they
fought and marched under banners. From a distance you could see
these banners and knew under whose kingly authority these armies
fought. You also knew to whom the glory and bounty in victory
would go. Every army marched under the authority of banners.

My relationship in Him is not just about feelings. His banners
speak of His kingly authority. His banners and authority has won a
bride in me. I move in Him especially under the one banner which
is blood red; although all the banners authenticate His life in me.

When I am distraught about the quality of my life and my ongoing failures of heart and soul, I place myself anew under His reigning

authority over me. I am not to be a drifter in this life. I have been purchased by His conquering everlasting love. In me, He has won a bride. I do not serve alone in this life. I move and live under His great authority and military. He positions me under His banners.

(See 1 Thessalonians 5:23; Exodus 17:15; Isaiah 25:6–9; Psalm 20:5.)

"Strengthen me with raisins, refresh me with apples, for I am faint with love" (2:5, NKJV)

After all this the soul nearly collapses! All natural energy which drove her is now gone. There is also so much misguided strength within me that truly needs weakening; personal energy which will never glorify Him. I have lived too long allowing my reactions to life drive me and control me.

In her relationship in Him she was not to spend her time running in and out of the dark tents followed by running in and out of His chambers. She is to rest now and begin her journey of learning to abide in Him. For most of us, this requires a lifetime.

> *Father, teach me deeply about You; Your presence, Your chambers and Your wine house. May Your new life unleashed from the tomb become a dynamic reality within me. In truth, Your cross and that sealed tomb were far more about me than You. May I truly come to know who You are to me, as well as the present day dynamic of Your love fully experienced in my life.*

> Abide in me and I in you, as a branch cannot bear fruit by itself, neither can you unless you abide in me.
>
> —JOHN 15:4

(See Psalm 28: 8–9; Isaiah 40: 29.)

"His left hand is under my head, and his right hand embraces me" (2:6, NKJV)

All that was strong within her, that which caused her to cry out, "Kiss me! Draw me! Tell me!" is now utter weakness. Also the strength of the dark tents has no hold on her.

He alone sustains her with His left hand and His right hand. The left hand represents the judicial ruling hand of God. His standards of holiness will reign in His kingdom and by the guidance of this King she is at rest in this.

She now has accepted with all her being the force of His strength. This is not a clench, but a godly embrace filling her life with a quality of purity she has never before experienced. He brings this to her. She did not bring it to Him.

His right hand represents His powerful strength at work in all the dimensions of her personal life. He is indeed her Savior, and He fulfills all that God, His father, requires of His people in His kingdom reign.

His arms create enormous strength in her, and at this time she expresses utter weakness and collapses into these arms. Her inner needs no longer drive her. He reigns supreme, and because of this enormous peace, she now sleeps. Her divine rest enhances her ability to learn to lean, learn to trust, and completely rest in Him. On becoming His bride she must learn to lean on Him, perhaps more in Him.

> *Oh, God, I welcome Your gift of rest to change my no's into yes's to You. Oh, God, I welcome this gift of rest You give to Your people. It is the first gift You give us in chamber love. You don't drive us out to work first and to prove our faith in You.*
>
> *It is not a rest apart from the knowledge of the living God, but a rest full of Your Son's presence. This divine rest enhances our ability to trust Him at all costs. It is a foundation for our personal faith to rest upon.*

Let us therefore strive to enter that rest, that no one fall by the same sort of disobedience.

—HEBREWS 4:11

The Lord is my strength and my song; he has become my salvation, Hark, glad songs of victory in the tents of the righteous; the right hand of the Lord does valiantly, the right hand of the Lord is exalted, the right hand of the Lord does valiantly.

—PSALM 118:14–16

My soul clings to thee; thy right hand upholds me.

—PSALM 63:8

(See Matthew 11:28–39; Psalm 108:6, 139:10, 23:1–3; Acts 17:27–28; Jude 1:24–25.)

"I charge you, O daughters of Jerusalem, by the gazelles or the does of the field, do not stir up nor awaken love until it pleases" (2:7, NKJV)

In the commentaries of The Song there is a general disagreement as to who is saying this. My heart says that God is. He is active in the pursuit of a bride for His glorious Son. His eye has always been on each of us. But in never perceiving His passion, we might live out our faith in general ambivalence towards Him or in utter ignorance in that this message at all concerns us. He has chosen a bride and we now stand on center stage.

She's not now His bride, but in the presence of His glory she is moving in that direction. His glory flowing over her and into her transforms her as it does us. She is now positioned in His right and in His left hand. She's now ready for the dance. But first comes total rest.

Concerning this lady He says, "Do not disturb in any way!" This first song now ends. She is submerged into His presence and her love for Him is not to be challenged nor interrupted until she pleases. How much time will pass until the beginning of the next song? We don't know. It's in her hands, and we wait.

The anxiety and damage from the dark tents drove her to cry out to Him. But this season has ended. Nothing is to disturb the soul's total rest in Him. This rest contains a deeper knowledge of Him. It is a holy collapse!

In working for Him we experience enormous weariness all the time. So, big deal! Yes, big deal! This song is created to romance us, which is to permeate every fragment of who we are, in the same way a powerful beautiful fragrance of His presence will begin to saturate us body, soul, and spirit. His kisses will open the doors for far more.

The soul from the dark tents is not being lectured to. No, at this time, this soul is being saturated by the presence of the living God. The knowledge now being imparted is not academic. It's a dynamic flow of life featured in the full presence of the Godhead.

> Be still and know that I am God.
>
> —Psalm 46:10

It is knowledge poured forth from those kisses. Pure intimacy has kissed this soul from the dark tents. How in the world does this take place? I believe the living God can't help Himself. He has waited a long time for this individual to desire Him.

> Thou dost show me the path of life; in thy presence there is fullness of joy; In thy right hand are pleasures for evermore.
>
> —Psalm 16:11

> Kiss me with the kisses of your mouth. For your love is better than wine, your anointing oils are fragrant. Your name is oil poured out; therefore the maidens love you.
>
> —Song of Solomon 1:2–3, rsv

Song Two

Come Away, My Love

2:8–3:5

Aᴿᴇ ᴡᴇ ᴄᴀʟʟᴇᴅ essentially to do or to be? Within His song we are drawn so close to our God we become authentic worshipers. I then suspect we cannot tell the difference between the two—doing and being.

God hungers for those who will worship Him body, soul, and spirit. The heavenly Father searches for those who will worship in spirit and in truth. He has opened all the doors to create this possibility within us. Without His glorious beauty and tenacious love, it would not be possible. I suspect worship and married love are inherently connected.

She now tells us what He is saying to her. We are very much like the spectators in Song One. She has so much to teach us.

Faith is our response in receiving and hearing His voice. I called the first song "Chamber Love." He was the one who lavished the wealth of His presence on her, and the only thing she did was to absorb and soak. But that was all she was expected to do. I wonder if the only right thing she ever did was to search precisely for Him. He expresses His great love and desire for her not in terms of principles, but in the fullness of His presence.

He demanded nothing. He simply lavished upon her His Father's heart. This experience was so intense, it overcame her. It weakened her into a state of complete rest in Him. A rest of dependency! Right

47

where He wanted her! She certainly was in no condition to conquer the world. But then again, maybe she was.

Now the call on her life has changed. It is a new season and a new revelation. The focus is "come away."

"The voice of my beloved. Behold, he comes, leaping upon the mountains, bounding over the hills" (2:8)

She has little understanding as to who He really is. She only knows His wonderful presence in Song One. She is still soaking in this great revelation of heart and soul—something we all could do.

Revelation is not merely a passing thought but more so a solid connection into His dynamic person. But alas, we need a quiet heart to perceive this. Her heart now is amazingly quiet. In fact, in some ways it is deathly quiet. Some things which drove her are now stone cold, quiet, amen. King David says:

> He restores my soul.
>
> —Psalm 23:3

> Truly, truly I say to you, he who hears my word and believes Him who sent me, has eternal life; he does not come into judgment, but has passed from death into life.
>
> —John 5:24

In Song One we left her in complete rest. There is nothing she can do to deserve His love, to deserve this sublime relationship. Nothing! Except to receive, and then pursue. He has loved her unconditionally!

She must first experience for herself soaking in agape love. In her future it will be required of her. She is ultimately called to both: doing and being. But He makes it genuine.

(See Romans 10:17.)

"Behold, he comes" (2:8)

"Behold, He comes." His love is a conquering love for He is a powerful Savior. He is a leaper. There is nothing that He cannot leap, except our complacency.

"No thanks, not much interested in anything you have to offer to me." We all struggle with this. He will surround us in every way possible, but He will respect our freedom of choice. Who will we serve? Who do we adore? And, ultimately, what will we choose to worship?

> *Lord, sometimes I wish You would not allow us this freedom.*
>
> *But called as Your bride and created in the Father's image allows me this power to choose. Please help me to want more of You. Please create in me a heart of hunger towards You. Lord, I am on the journey, but I am feeble."*

(See John 5:24; Romans 6:5, 6:23, 8:1–2; 2 Timothy 3:10.)

"The voice of my beloved, behold he comes" (2:8)

Christianity is a faith founded on revelation. God is revealed to us through His Son, Jesus Christ. Or else we would have no idea what God is like. We'd be clueless! The idols we collect, or create, attest to this fact.

The hunger of God is that we know Him, as well as enjoy Him. Revelation means making a mystery understandable to us, but normally not all at once. Our relationship in Him requires time, producing inner growth. Revelation, producing faith is tied into a vibrant, loving person, not simply a dogma.

He lives and breathes! He is the most strategic power in our world! He is full of life! The dynamic of His beautiful person surrounds us! He could never just sit on a shelf encased in stone. The apostle Paul explains Him this way:

> And the grace of our Lord overflowed for me with the
> faith and love that are in Jesus Christ.
>
> —1 Timothy 1:14

Truth in Scripture is not simply abstract knowledge as in a theory or in a principle, otherwise it would only require mental ascension.

Truth, for us, breathes!

Truth, personally speaks to me. He knows where I am. He knows my name, and He calls me "most beautiful among women." He's after my heart, the center of my being. I want Him to have it, "Oh, Lover of my soul."

(See 1 Corinthians 4:1; 2 Corinthians 5:16–21; John 14:6, 4:24–25; Romans 8:21; 1 John 2:27.)

"The voice of my beloved, behold he comes, bounding over the hills" (2:8)

There is nothing He cannot leap. It describes His great glory. In His chamber she experienced personal love at the deepest level. Oh, how she first needed His love, drenched in perfect acceptance of all that she is, broken and lost. His favor is utter comfort, and the result is that she slept. Perfect rest creates perfect faith.

Sin and a soul adrift do not define who I am before the Father's heart. My wholeness and new life in Christ does. I stand in Him before the living God, a new creation in Christ. Jesus leaped the enormous mountain of complacency rooted in unbelief, within me.

> Therefore, if anyone is in Christ, he is a new creation;
> the old has passed away, behold the new has come.
> —2 CORINTHIANS 5:17

(See Revelation 3:20–22; Colossians 3:1–4; 2 Corinthians 5:17; Romans 5:4.)

"Leaping upon the mountains, bounding over the hills" (2:8)

A new season in life ushers in new revelations. It's time to move forth from His comfortable chambers into some mountain leaping.

Our faith, our relationship in Christ, is not frozen. Because He's not static! But so often personal doubts lodged within us from the old life serve as the foundations for our inner walls.

So He's the mountain leaper to reach us, to save us, and birth within us the knowledge of the living God. He leaped every possible barrier between us and the heart of His Father. He desires to move even closer to her. Mountain leaping is all about Him.

In this new season she is to learn to leap and dance over those barriers and hurdles within her.

In giving Him a sacrifice of praise in my heart, I am allowing Him to form within me leaping feet. I know this pleases Him. It also ushers in the anointing of the Holy Spirit, which draws my praise into deeper worship. At this time, in Him, I am stronger and bigger than all of my mountains.

> Come let us go up to the mountain of the Lord, to the house of the God of Jacob; that he may teach us his ways and we may walk in his paths.
>
> —MICAH 4:2

(See Hebrews 10:7–10.)

"Behold, there he stands behind our wall, gazing in at the windows, looking through the lattice" (2:9)

She is peaking out through the latticework of her soul, which represents her incomplete knowledge of who He truly is in her life.

I say to Him, "Lord, blow out the obstructions in that lattice work creating her blindness of soul. Give her the whole load of revelation as the great mountain leaper of life. Give it all to her now! "

The Lord's desire is not to blow us away nor entertain us, but to secure us in Him on the heights. His desire is not to give us a "wow!" testimony, but a solid personal knowledge of who He is. Our soul best handles a little at a time, or our wandering hearts will love and serve the "wow" and lose Him on the journey.

In the Hebrew, "gazing in," is powerful. His radiance blooms into her soul. It is a powerful heart-changing encounter.

He is moving as close to her as He can at this time. In His great glory He seeks her through her limited perceptions of their relationship. He now glows in radiance and fullness of light, and she is to know Him in this dimension. He is not just any old mountain leaper. He is calling her forth into complete transformation.

> *How free we want You to be in us. Yes, we desire the "wow" and the radiance of Your fullness of life. Work in us because our faith so often sinks into a religious habit. We exalt You in the working out of our lives, and we love Your patience with us. Take Your time in us. I will dance with You in the high places.*

(See 2 Corinthians 3:17–18, 4:6; Lamentations 3:24–25.)

"My beloved speaks and says to me" (2:10)

A new season commands new revelation. It's time to mountain leap! Why? Because that's what He's doing! In my own faith walk I realized that I did not expect new revelation, new insights of His person, especially not in my life. This word awakens my soul and sharpens my spirit to His Spirit. In this context of relationship in Him, my knowledge and personal expectations begin to soar!

He now has a different address. But the chambers were His address. The chambers, or the wine house, are simply the beginning of revealing to us His marvelous presence. Because our faith eyes are so confined to regimented focus, we miss so much about who He is personally to each of us. His presence is always an unfolding of His person. Now it's about the high places. A new season, increased revelation, and subsequently of whom she is to become.

She must learn to contend with the barriers and walls which were allowed to define who she is. How often I've prayed, "Oh, Lord, take this and that away! Make my life easier! Please!" A common prayer He has seldom answered. The human condition is rarely changed in "nice and easy." But as His presence expands, she changes.

In this new season she is to learn to leap and to dance over those barriers and hurdles. It ushers in the anointing of the Holy Spirit which draws my praise into deep worship. I grow stronger and bigger than all of my mountains. I possess hind's feet similar to His, for He is like a gazelle or a young stag. This new dimension has been added into my life because of who He is. All my personal expectations are changing.

(See Psalm 23; 2 Samuel 22:17–20, 32–34.)

"My beloved speaks and says to me" (2:10)

He is intensely personal. He will win my heart sometime in my life. At least this is what I hope for.

He speaks to us. We come fully equipped with built-in receiving sets, the human heart. This is true for all of us. When we give Him our hearts, these sets are activated by His Spirit. By studying Scripture we grow to recognize His voice.

We don't fully understand what it all means to be created in God's image. So God not only gives us a personal Savior, but He has also been appointed as the Lover of our souls. He is not simply a trainer who walks with us, but He adorns us with a Savior's manner of loving.

> *How tenderly you love me. You will one day judge my life, but first you seek to love me into your beautiful wholeness. How you search after me. Your love will not let me go. Your love will not fail me.*

> O Lord, thou has searched me and known me. Thou knowest when I sit down and when I rise up; thou discern my thoughts from afar.
>
> —Psalm 139:1–2

(See John 5:8; Philippians 3:10; 1 John 2:5, 3:19, 24, 5:13, 20; Matthew 13:16 Psalm 8:3–9.).

"Arise my love, my fair one and come away" (2:10)

His word to her is to "come away and spend time with me." Shouldn't He test her faith and send her out on a service mission first? How often I learned as a new Christian that if I truly loved Christ, then I prove it by serving Him. Not a bad message but perhaps out of order.

A new revelation creates a deeper relationship. The more we experience and know of Him, the more will be given to us and thus required of us. As our hearts move with Him, we will love all that He has become within us.

But perhaps for now, He knocks.

> Behold I stand at the door and knock; if anyone hears my voice and opens the door, I will come into him, and eat with him, and he with me. He who conquers, I will grant him to sit with me on my throne, as I myself conquered and sat down with my Father on his throne. He who has an ear, let him hear what the Spirit says to the churches.
>
> —REVELATION 3:20–22

He presses in to draw us more deeply into His high places. But for now He bends down to ignite this mighty revelation through the latticework of our incomplete faith, and then He waits.

> *O Lover of my soul, knock down all my doors! Get my attention! Draw me after You! Enable my fragile heart to press hard after You!*

"Arise, my love, my fair one, and come away" (2:10)

At this point she is fully satisfied with her journey in faith. He is leaping, and she is sitting in utter contentment. She is delighted in seeing Him. He is glorious! But in her present state she still sits. She behaves so much like us.

> *Your blessings and gifts are marvelous. But must I move on? Can I not pursue You on my terms and in my way? Probably not.*

She now displays no urgency to press on into His glorious leaping presence.

I said to the Lord, "You leap all these hindrances and obstacles in our lives to reach our hearts. So, good grief, leap the lattice work and get her out of there."

He answered. "That, I will not do. She is to move in complete freedom in me. I am calling her not only as a chosen servant, but also as my bride—not as my slave. I do not enslave. I have paid to set her free, and she is indeed that. I honor her choices."

So in His great glory He bounds over the hills and mountains, puts on his brakes, bends down, and speaks lovingly to her, on her terms. This is the One we seek to draw closer to—a gentle Lover of our souls.

(See John 10:10; 2 Corinthians 4:15; Ephesians 3:20.).

"And come away" (2:10)

The Song puts the focus on the heart, not on the works. Too often the central focus on the teachings we have heard has been about works. But,

> Faith without works is dead.
>
> —James 2:17

But so often our works look shabby and ordinary.

Abraham is an example of dynamic works in offering up his son to the living God. His work is tied into to his personal relationship with the living God. The fact that Abraham was willing to offer his son shows that the living God has his trust as well as his heart.

From the beginning God has sought her heart. She was hungry to be loved by Him. But, yet, He and His father were hungrier to fill her heart with the intimate knowledge of all that He is. There is so much more she is to experience in Christ and it involves the high places. His call for more of her promises a greater revelation of His love for her.

"For lo the winter is past, the rain is over and gone" (2:11)

Winter, for fruit trees, is a season of enormous activity, but it all takes place in the root system; the hidden life of the heart and soul. Without this established inner strength, there would be no fruit, poor fruit, or at most a very small harvest.

That special time spent in His chambers was her winter. Old roots had to die, and an entirely new system was beginning its development. Her rest, or inactivity in His presence, was performing within her a great interior work. That season was appointed to rest in Him, not to mountain leaping.

> *Father, teach me Your ways and what You desire to create in me. I so often watch others in other seasons and want exactly what they have. I then miss the great work You desire to see accomplished within me. Create within me a contentment to become what You desire. O Lord, teach me your ways and to quietly experience Your tender love.*

(See Galatians 5:22; Matthew 7:16–19; John 15.)

"The flowers appear on the earth, the time of singing has come, and the voice of the turtle dove is heard in our land" (2:12)

In His eyes He sees beauty developing within her. How did this happen? Gardens need tilling, lots of nourishment, and careful planting. Developing a beautiful flower garden requires a great deal of work and commitment.

How did this occur? She just slept! I didn't see any personal sweat equity on her part in this project. No, she just simply collapsed in the arms of heaven's master gardener. On the outside as one looking in, this season in her life appears unproductive. But it produced His loveliness and fragrance within her person. A season of rest in Him created divine beauty.

(See Numbers 24:2–6; Jeremiah 31:12–14.)

"The time of singing has come" (2:12)

The time of blooming, as well as singing is here. I suspect these two activities are well connected. We are a singing people within a singing faith. Unfortunately, we have so often come to view our singing simply as a form of personal entertainment. Too often it is only presented to us in this context. We essentially sing to make us feel good, and it does. The Holy Spirit uses music to draw us more deeply into personal worship. In worshiping the living God, our hearts are changed.

Our God loves music. Right now in His presence is great music. The announcement of the birth of His Son was presented to some sleepy shepherds by the greatest concert in history—I am sure, engraved within them body, soul, and spirit. For the rest of their lives, they spoke of this to anyone who would listen.

Our God loves music in revealing His great heart to His people. In her future there will be much singing and a great overflow of His joy. After all, this is a song we are looking at.

(See Ephesians 5:19; Colossians 3:16; James 5:13; 1 Corinthians 14:15.)

"The voice of the turtle dove is now heard in our land" (2:12)

This voice is calling forth a mate. His voice is calling forth His bride from within her. He has chosen her, but she was the first to choose Him. Or was she? He has had His eye on her for a very long time. He saw her in those fields, as well as a member of the Kedar family whose lifestyle rejected everything His kingdom reign stands for.

He came to earth to give us an honest choice concerning our eternal destiny. Before this we had no choices. Dark tents don't offer any. They simply inscribe within us darkness.

(See John 10:10; 14:5.)

"The fig tree puts forth its figs" (2:13)

Jesus compared Israel a number of times to a fig tree. He judged her fruitlessness. She certainly had established an impressive religion with massive rules and regulations, which only suggested spiritual life; but comparatively drab to Moses' life, in which he enjoyed the spectacular presence of the living God in a portable tent. But in Israel's temples there was little glory of God's presence. There was no production of either His vines or his figs. There was no heavenly life flow.

Today we *are* those portables tents. Moses enjoyed God's Shekinah glory. Will our tents ever enjoy this depth of His presence? I suspect one day we will.

God uses the fig tree over and over again, as either a metaphor of His great blessing and presence in a nation, or of His great judgment on a nation. There is sweetness from this fruit that nourishes man both within and without. This lady has also been nourished in the strength and sweetness of His fervent presence. She said, "Draw me," and oh, He did!

> *Lord, I am that tree. Too often there is no authentic sweetness or personal substance of strength within me. My life seldom produces the figs of Your rich presence. Please help me see a change here! I know this is on Your heart as well.*

> For figs are not gathered from thorns, nor grapes picked from the bramble bush. The good man out of the good treasure of his heart produces good, and the evil man out of his evil treasure produces evil.
>
> —Luke 6:44–45

(See Jeremiah 13:8; Mark 13:28; Exodus 40:34–38; Psalm 3:3–4; Deuteronomy 5:24.)

"And the vines are in blossom; they give forth fragrance" (2:13)

> I am the vine, you are the branches. He who abides in me, and I in him, he it is that Bears much fruit, for apart from me you can do nothing.
>
> —John 15:5

The entire fifteenth chapter of John is this unusual message. Jesus was teaching His disciples this amazing truth just before He was to bear our cross, descend into hell, and subsequently ascend into heaven. A journey He said yes to on our behalf. But at this time the disciples had no clue as to what was about to take place and how their relationship to Him would radically change.

In relationship with Him as God's vine appointed to our lives, we not only possess a glorious knowledge of Him, but we also now wear His personal fragrance. Fragrance is mentioned often in The Song. A life which bears His alluring fragrance will attract and soften adjacent hearts. Our hearts are created to enjoy life in Him. His manifested fragrance softens the heart to receive Him. This heavenly fragrance has enormous drawing power.

For us, bearing divine fruit should not always be a rigid outward struggle, but more an experience rooted in rest. God the Father as well as God the Son are very active in the personal growth of their vineyards.

> *Father, forgive me that I seem to live out my daily routine so often in utter ignorance of all the energy You direct into my life. I thank You that Jesus is the vine, and I am connected into Him through enormous grace. Please help me to discern and welcome Your powerful presence in me. The vineyard You produce is beautiful, healthy, and bountiful. Thank You! I welcome you into my life.*

(See John 15.)

"Arise, my love, my fair one, and come away" (2:3)

The call is repeated. Praise God, He repeats Himself! He does this often in Scripture. He knows how weak and unfocused we are. He understands who we are, and where we are, and yet He still calls us to Himself. Amen!

He is focused on her, and He will not let her go. Oh, praise God, He is the tenacious Lover of our souls! After all, He still calls her "My love!"

These are words directed into my heart as well, for this song has been written for my benefit.

You replace in me that which I lack. This word of Your fruit and fragrances appointed into my life birth a faith in me to never let You go. But, Lord, I still do! Fill me anew with that which You alone can provide in me, Oh, Lover of my soul. Because of your enormous grace and depth of love, You will have a bride in me. It is truly about You, more than it is about me.

(See Psalms 16:5–6, 73:23–26; Jeremiah 31:3; Luke 1:38; John 4:14, 10:27–30, 14:27, 17:2; Romans 8:32.)

"O my dove, in the clefts of the rock, in the covert of the cliff, let me see your face, let me hear your voice, for your voice is sweet, and your face is comely" (2:14)

The voice of the Father speaks and, oh, how personal He is! He longs for my voice and my face, and He knows my name. He is up close and personal and, oh, how He desires that I seek Him in the same quality of commitment! He waits for me.

The metaphor "clefts of the rock" points me to draw away, or draw aside, in Him. In doing this, I choose to make Him special in my life.

In the last section of Song One, she said little to nothing about her inner "me." The Song began with "kiss me, draw me, and tell me." And it was appropriate; but then the "me," issue seemed deathly quiet. Now in Song Two, it's His heart crying out for more of her, thus more of me.

The call for her presence has deepened. The call is now to the clefts of the rock in the high places where eagles live. She first called to Him; and now in return, He calls to her, "Come away, let me see your face and hear your sweet voice. Come away! "

(See Psalms 57:1–2, 59:16–17; Isaiah 28:15; Hebrews 6:18.)

"Let me see your face" (2:14)

His call for her heart is now far more intense. This is the voice of God speaking, "Let me see your face." The heart of the Father hungers for His people. His heart aches in that His people know so little about His presence in their daily routines. In not knowing Him at this level of affection, they subsequently do not seek Him.

It was imperative the lady, who began the entire song, desired first to seek His face. She first cried out for intimacy. But remember, He wrote her words through the mind of Solomon. No doubt a precious truth, which will change our hearts, is that He first seeks and hungers for us—not only in the swift passage of time throughout our days, but in the clefts of the rock which are a strong safe place for us to rest in.

(See Numbers 6:25; Psalm 17:15.)

"Let me see your face" (2:14)

"Oh, be careful that you don't become so heavenly minded that you are no earthly good." I have heard this unfortunate statement all of my life. Heavenly mindedness is no longer a problem anymore. It is almost nonexistent! But The Song is now making it an issue. The heart pursuing Him is now willing to hang out with Him body, soul, and spirit.

The clefts of the rock are impossible for a carnal heart to reach, but easy in the power of God's Holy Spirit. She is to rise up and experience the treasure of those cliffs, those hidden places from the world.

His hunger to draw her closer into Himself is not simply to make greater demands of her. She is not essentially called to serve Him, but to be fully loved by Him. Her future service will be birthed out of this intimacy of heart.

Even from the very beginning of life in conception, His Spirit brooded over her. His Father's heart was thrilled in that her heart would someday embody His glory—a destiny appointed to each one of us.

The two actors which participated in her conception possibly could not have cared less. In fact they may have considered her as nothing more than an unfortunate *accident*, a word expressing the value of her birth throughout her lifetime. But in the heavenly places, her birth brought shouts of praise!

She is now on the blessed journey as to the deeper meaning of who she is. Her conception rooted her in the dark tents of Kedar. But her thirst for the living God, her true Father, brought her into his divine escape route.

This scripture now calling to her is so full of the Father's pleasure! It bursts forth in enormous passion! "Arise my love and enjoy all I have for you!" (author's paraphrase).

> *Father, You understand how darkness can leave a deep stain within us creating deaf ears and heart blindness. Have patience with us and our children, and all who we love. Keep calling and we will come.*

(See Mark 1:2; Matthew 7:2; Acts 2:25; 2 Corinthians 3:18, 4:6.)

"Let me hear your voice, for your voice is sweet, and your face is lovely" (2:14, NKJV)

> *And what would You like to hear? What would please You?*

The Psalmists will teach us. They teach us the concepts, the phrases, as well as the words of praise and worship to please Him.

> Bless the Lord, O my soul; and all that is within me, bless his holy name. Bless the Lord, O my soul, and forget not all his benefits, who forgives all your iniquity, who heals all your diseases, who redeems your life from the pit, who crowns you with steadfast love and mercy.
>
> —PSALM 103:1–4

He strongly desires to hear my thoughts, expressed personally in the way I choose to pray. He knows my voice as I indeed grow to know His. It is not His desire, as it would not be ours, for a nanny to tell us what our children are saying. No, we want to hear their voices for ourselves and see the expressions on their faces. He is no different!

The "draw nears" in the Book of Hebrews echo the same sentiment. Just as I am, I am called to spend time in the holy of holies by the new and living way opened up to me, to experience the love of God, a Father's heart, and to enjoy His presence as He enjoys mine.

This scripture is essentially saying to each of us today: "Come closer! Allow Me to become important in your life. Come closer! Know My voice and My ways and My hopes for you. Know what I have established on your behalf as well as your children's. Cross the distance between us, draw near. I've already bridged it. You are worth it to Me."

(See Hebrews 4:16; 7:19, 25; 10:1, 22; 11:6.)

"Catch us the foxes, the little foxes, that spoil the vineyards; for our vineyards are in blossom" (2:15)

She's in bloom. How in the world did this happen? I want to be in bloom too!

He now addresses personal problems concerning her little foxes. Fox families make their homes among the root system of the vines. The little ones, especially, dig around the new tender roots and chew on them. In doing this, these roots may be destroyed, and often times the entire vine suffers and dies.

The voice of God points this out, but she is neither being scolded nor condemned for her personal problems. This has never deterred Him from drawing her closer and closer to Himself. His word also dispels the myth that only those who are really spiritual are called to Him, only those who have their act together.

He said to her, "Catch us." It's a joint process. She's not being put into a self-improvement course. Her personal failings and weaknesses will find their strength "in Him."

This word is comforting and full of His grace. I don't begin to measure up in deserving His enormous love presence within me. I don't deserve this special attention. The seeds of my dark tents continue to affect a harvest within me. I don't deserve and I don't. He has chosen me, foxes and all!

That which He requires of me He will cultivate within me.

Holiness will be an authentic part of who I am. He makes me genuine. He truly is my soul's Lover.

(See Mark 4.)

"My beloved is mine and I am his, he pastures his flock among the lilies" (2:16)

Her confession of faith is beautiful. I will, morning after morning, make it mine as well. "Speak this into my heart and soul. I am bonded into intimacy with you."

My daily tantrums are my reactions to other grumpy people, problem children, the incessant voice of the media, etc., and so on. This is where I live out my faith in a daily relationship in Him.

A principle to respect is that He chooses to pasture His flock among the lilies, and not the thorn patches.

The beautiful lily always seems to be looking up. It always seems to be focused upon the heavenly places. Within the center of their form is a small cup which collects heaven's dew. This is heaven's refreshment and strength flowing into them. They always seek to be ready to receive from the presence of the Lord. Even their beauty is to glorify their Creator, and perhaps teach us as well. All the wealth and beauty of King Solomon did not compare to the beauty of God within a lily. Solomon understood this.

> Consider the lilies, how they grow; they neither toil nor spin.
>
> —Luke 12:27

Jesus said this. He's after lily growth within us. He's after the human heart.

Wake up in the morning slowly and quietly. Perceive and confess His presence. Discern His word to you for the day; for as you slept heaven's dew fell gently over your heart and soul. His word is encouraging and sweet.

You have given Him permission to be active in your life and this is simply one of the ways He chooses to do it. He frequently lavishes upon you His love. But this truth so often escapes us. Earthly life drowns it out.

(See Deuteronomy 32:2; Psalms 110:3, 133:3; Proverb 4:23; Isaiah 26:19; Micah 5:7; Matthew 6:28–29.)

"Be like a gazelle, or a young stag upon rugged mountains" (2:17)

Knowing Him only as one who adores her in Song One is not enough. God has appointed Him to be the Savior of our hearts and souls, and yet there is still far more to know about Him as Lord.

He's glorious and He owns the high places as well. She is not to go through life without knowing Him there.

But now He is not only the lamb of the gospels but He is also exalted as the High Priest of the tabernacle drawing God's people into the holy of holies. God ripped open that veil between Himself and those He loved. But even tabernacle closeness was not enough. But we're a defiled people. How can He draw us even closer?

He is the Lamb, High Priest, and yet still far more. He became the appointed King of heaven, and truly as the Bridegroom King of heaven. Who He is fully effects who we are called to be. As Bridegroom of our souls He draws us into the intimacy God's heart longs for.

He draws us into a love life in Him we never dreamed of. What's this song about? It's about this journey appointed to each of us, and it will lead us into the high places of His glory.

How could this ever be? It's His Father's heart which is longing for this relationship with His people. He will not leave us living in our sin and unbelief. He will continue to lovingly harass us to want more. Amen!

"Draw me after you, let us make haste" (1:4).

He will perfect this desire in her. After all, it was His beauty which birthed it within her heart. The Gospels draw us into the new birth, Jesus, the Lamb of God, opens up to us. But it is just a glorious beginning.

Thank you!

(See John 6:44–45; Psalm 45:15.)

"Until the day breathes and the shadows flee, turn, my beloved, be like a gazelle, or a young stag upon rugged mountains" (2:1)

The Song of Songs romances all that we are unto Him; and in response she now turns to Him and says, "No thanks, not now. Be on your way and do your thing." How in the world did this response find its way into this scripture?

> For freedom Christ has set us free; stand fast therefore and do not submit again to a yoke of slavery.
> —Galatians 5:1

The apostle Paul wrote this to the church. He was reacting to God's people becoming entangled within a religious system. He continues to say,

> For in Christ, what avails us is faith working through love.
> —Galatians 5:6

I am ultimately free to choose this deeper relationship with the Bridegroom of my soul. His great love and presence will never seek to enslave me into a system. I do have a choice here. His quality of freedom appointed unto my life, is authentic.

I have been called to the highest position in the heavenly places for His people; the bride of Christ. But it is very important to Him that I have complete freedom in this matter. She is not chained, nor dragged off. The other heavenly power prefers those tactics.

Only someone completely free can wear His glory. In the garden we see this in Christ just before His crucifixion. He was asking His Father about an alternative to His terrible cross. Is there not possibly another way? No, there wasn't! I don't think it was the suffering He was to experience which caused Him to seek this. I think it was the separation from God that caused Him to cry out,

My God, my God, why hast thou forsaken me?
—Matthew 27:46

(See John 8:32, 36; Romans 6:18, 22, 8:2; Galatians 5:1, 13.)

"Turn my beloved" (2:17)

What quality of Christ's presence do I desire as His potential bride? The Song is about His glorious Bridegroom presence within our hearts and manifested in every area of our lives. Bridegroom presence represents a marriage union.

In most of us our meager faith is not able to ascend into the living truth that He would desire this quality of union and intimacy within us. His beautiful glory is appointed to be revealed within us: body, soul, and spirit. Glory found in the high places. This is to be birthed personally, and then it overflows our human limits. Bridal status is established not only for the individual believer but then unto His glorious body.

She does not grasp this at this point in her development. She is still overwhelmed by what she does understand concerning her relationship in Him. So she makes her choice: no to coming away with Him into the high places, and yes to comfortably staying put.

The apostle Paul prays this for Christ's body:

> That the God of our lord Jesus Christ, the Father of glory, may give you a spirit of wisdom and of revelation in the knowledge of him, having the eyes of your hearts enlightened, that you may know what is the hope to which he has called you, what are the riches of his glorious inheritance in the saints, and what is the immeasurable greatness of his power in us who believe.
> —Ephesians 1:17–19

In a relationship such as this, He is so pleased to allow a flow of personal revelation to touch and change our hearts. It includes a flow of sweet affection in changing us body, soul, and spirit.

(See Romans 4:6; Acts 26:18; Romans 16:25–27; Ephesians 1:9–23.)

"Upon my bed by night I sought him whom my soul loves; I sought him but found him not. I called him, but he gave no answer" (3:1)

His presence sustained her. He's now gone! Her freedom of choice resulted in the loss of enormous personal pleasure and comfort. How could she desire anything else?

I suspect her choice was more focused upon her love of the great comfort zone He provided for her. What she now desires will not define nor produce a deeper relationship in Him. What she now desires is too little, and The Song opens this up for us. The lattice metaphor suggests we only possess a very limited personal knowledge of who He is.

"But it's enough. My heart is satisfied," she says.

In this scripture there is no sense of holy abandonment, even though she may have deserved it. There is no sense of condemnation. The wrath of heaven is not evident. He simply withdraws His discernable presence, for a season. The journey of her heart has just begun. It will not end here, in a poor choice.

"I've lost grace! I've lost Him! I've lost His pleasure! How could He ever love me again? I am truly a family disgrace!" None of these articulated emotions are in this passage. They follow us out of darkness.

But consider: what's it going to take to cause me to hunger for more of Him? More was offered but she was fully gratified. She loved what she knew of Him, and it was enough.

He will direct these seasons in our lives to develop within us not only running legs, but leaping legs. In Revelation 3:20 He stands at the door and knocks. He does not beat it down. This is not His style of manifested grace. He will now draw her to Himself through her own personal choices.

We all experience seasons of spiritual dryness. They make us thirsty. These seasons are not only frustrating and discouraging, but they also create within us intense desires to know Him more deeply, and to enjoy Him more fully.

(See Matthew 5:33, 7:7; Luke 12:29–30; John 6:26–27; Isaiah 30:18.)

"I called Him, but he gave no answer" (3:1)

This is a common experience. Heaven's door is shut, and we are on the outside! Indeed, the door is never shut to His children but a time of silence may be in order. Too much is a stake!

In great enjoyment of heart and soul, she prospered in His chambers. Oh, it was great! More and more of chamber love is what she desires. And He does give her more, so much more!

If we cry out, "More from You!" then He must have more of us. Personal faith waivers if it is not connected into vibrant revelation. A great adjustment is needed. Neither one is seeking something casual. No, the goal is married love in the heavenly places.

She calls, and He did not answer. She assumes He's obviously changed His mind concerning her as a future bride. No, quite the opposite is true! She is very much on His mind. He needs to see something deeper happen within her. He now appoints her to a season of silence.

> For everyone who asks receives, and he who seeks finds,
> and to him who knocks it will be opened.
> —MATTHEW 7:8

This scripture tells us our search will never be in vain. But it does not tell us that it will be on our terms, and within our preferred seasons. He is Lord and His intense desire is that we know Him intimately. He desires a Bridegroom relationship.

I suspect we really don't have a clue as to what this is all about. But this is good! His purpose steers us in the direction of personal experience, not simply the comprehension of a good idea.

It's time to desire deeper things so the sweet revelation of His presence is withdrawn. His personal word is silent, and He waits, and she now pursues.

> I love those who love me, and those who seek me diligently find me.
> —PROVERBS 8:17

More of Him does require more of us on His terms.

(See Deuteronomy 4:29; Ezra 8:22; Psalms 9:10, 53:1, 119:2.)

"I will rise now and go about the city, in the streets and in the squares; I will seek him whom my soul loves. I sought him but found him nought" (3:2)

Where is she directing her search? The city, the streets, and the squares all speak of the environment of the natural life, which suggests only natural strength. He, however, did become fully man to partake of our humanity. He is very acquainted with the scenario of the natural habitats of mind and soul.

But the blatant result is, she found Him not. How serious is she? Is she willing to come to grips with the results? Natural life insists that He reveal Himself on her terms, and this may be the problem.

We basically live out so much of our lives in our city squares and streets. By inhabiting these places we allow them the power to define us.

He seeks to reestablish within her a deeper revelation of her destiny in Him. But as His people and His beautiful purpose appointed unto our lives, we remain genuinely bereft of this knowledge. It's now the season for His appointed high places. This place in Him authenticates and redefines who we really are. But she said, "No, not interested!" How often we mimic the same no!

We, as well, are appointed to a heavenly destiny while our lives are under the influence, and often guidance, of the city streets of our culture. This song is awakening us into these truths, not simply to be understood, but to be lived out. He is not a theory, nor a principle. He is vibrant flowing truth as the river described in the Psalms.

> They feast on the abundance of thy house, and thou
> givest them drink, from the river of thy delights.
>
> —Psalm 36:8

But how do we then grasp this? In His presence!

Wake up my heart. He is proposing to me, the creature of the city streets. I say yes to You, Bridegroom of my soul. I know it is feeble and my yes drowns in the unbelief of my surroundings. That's who I am. But I suspect You know all of this. The journey of becoming your bride is fully appointed unto my life, and I say, "Yes! Yes! Yes! Yes! "

(See Psalm 36.)

"I sought him and found him not" (3:2)

She found Him not? How serious is she? Is she willing to come to grips with these results? Natural life insists that He reveal Himself on her terms, and this is the problem. Growing in faith requires from us a certain amount of seeking.

Another woman described in John 4, as the woman at the well, made a tiring trip in the hottest hour of the day to Jacob's well in Samaria. She was one thirsty lady! She was determined to get water!

At this well she met heaven's well. His Father directed Jesus, as His well, to wait in the full heat of that day, to meet her. The Christ, the Lord of heaven, was thirsty too! This divine appointment produced glorious results in this woman nobody wanted. Her disastrous life was the driest well on earth.

This woman was a member of a nation who years before said a huge no to the living God by choosing idolatry over Him. Their lives were disastrous! I suspect she truly represented the lives of these people. The Jews hated the Samaritans! But the heart of God sent His thirsty Son to them by meeting this disgusting woman. She was neither spiritual nor lovely.

> Jesus answered her, 'If you knew the gift of God, and who it is that is saying to you, 'give me a drink,' you would have asked him and he would have given you living water.'"
>
> —John 4:10

The glory of the presence of the Lord was manifested that hot dry day, and we receive a profound revelation because of her. Her personal encounter with living water impacted that same nation.

The Father's heart is thirsty and seeking. He hungers for those who will worship Him in spirit and in truth. In this way we come to know Him deeply. As He called the woman of The Song to Himself in the high places, this is what He desired to perfect within her.

On my own I am not capable of worshiping Him. Living water is a glorious revelation of heaven's purpose appointed unto the Samaritan woman's life. Somewhere deep within the woman of the well was the enormous potential of a worshiping heart. That day she met another well, full and flowing with life.

God is not about to casually let go of the woman of The Song. Her relationship rooted in Him will not be about silence. Great revelation and the wealth of His presence is the prize. But at this time she does not know this. He is very much aware of where she is and what she is doing.

(See John 4:7–42.)

"The watchmen found me, as they went about the city. Have you seen him whom my soul loves?" (3:3)

God has appointed watchmen in His church. They are those who understand the high places and have a sound vision of safety and nourishment for God's people. They comprise our pastors and teachers. There is no sense in The Song that the journey of the heart is essentially solitary. In 1:8 He says to her,

> If you don't know, most beautiful among women, follow
> in the tracks of the flock, and pasture your kids beside
> the shepherd's tent.
>
> —Song of Songs 1:8

The journey of the heart is essentially a personal journey but it is to be pursued in the context of God's people. We all face confusion of soul, hardness of hearing, and coldness of heart on this journey. These are the normal demises of the human heart. It's here while on earth we begin this journey, but the ramifications reach far into the heavenly places. This journey of the heart is well worth it, and it is never in vain.

"Scarcely had I passed them, when I found him whom my soul loves, held him and would not let him go until I had brought him into my mother's house, and into the chambers of her that conceived me" (3:4)

It's done! She found Him! The search is finished!

It's not a casual encounter. Her heart was increasingly stirred up to find Him. Her personal loss was too great.

No, it's an open door to a glorious beginning. Her personal journey has now a fresh start into the deeper revelations of the Lover of her soul.

She held Him and would not let Him go. The season of His silence worked this strength within her. This second song now amazingly ends in her embrace. It was His embrace at the end of the first song, it was not a clench. But possibly hers is. The Lord loves our cleaving to Him.

The time of solitude alone on her bed exposed her to enormous emptiness. God will allow us these experiences to ignite within us an intensely searching heart. She put all her effort into seeking to restore her relationship in Him. Her searching, at best, may have not been in all the right places, but He was intent that she eventually find Him. She had to be serious about this but the searching was guarded by heavenly beings. It was not all left up to her. He would not lose her.

> *Oh, heart of mine, learn and listen. Teach me about cleaving. Redirect the dreams within me which lead me into the city streets. Lovingly change all that embraces me and defines me, into a heart more serious about You, O You, whom my soul loves.*

> To thee they cried, and were saved; in thee they trusted, and were not disappointed.
>
> —Psalm 22:5

(See Psalms 22:1–5, 9:12, 145:19; 2 Samuel 22:7.)

"Until I brought him into my mother's house, and into the chamber of her that conceived me" (3:4)

She cried out to Him with all her heart for His divine kisses of intimacy. "Draw me away, and I will come, Oh, Lover of my soul. Tell me, You whom my soul loves, where You pasture Your flock and make it lie down at noon" (author paraphrase). This all describes the intensity of her heart.

Those dark tents have a strong hold on her. They defined her and directed her life. What does it take to change all of this? Now is the time to enter back into the roots of her beginnings. Family lines are rooted into different belief systems and particular appetites, which draw us away from the living God. Now is the time to address this in her life.

She holds Him tight and now a visit into her mother's house is necessary—her mother's chambers, womb, household, family line, roots. Their power will not direct her future. Her embrace of Him now requires a deeper work.

We are tethered to our families. It is God's plan for our lives to begin there. We don't harshly judge or reject them for the care, or lack of, that formed us. We forgive and bring our family line within the power and influence of Him whom our soul loves. We now love them in newness of life and become for them a life flow of grace. When this happens the tethers no longer control us. Her past is now fully connected in Him and her future is set free to fly.

(See Ephesians 4:22–24; 2 Corinthians 5:17; Romans 6:4; Colossians 3:10.)

"I adjure you, o daughters of Jerusalem, by the gazelles or the hinds of the field, that you stir not up nor awaken love until it pleases" (3:5)

The second song now ends with the same word as in the first song. First is a strong warning to those who are in her company examining her life. They see dramatic changes taking place, but they know Him not.

In some ways they are us. We have not taken this journey in

pursuing intimacy in Christ, and for this reason God created this poetic woman to teach us. This call to intimacy is to every ear who will receive it.

We need to understand what He knows about us and how we are to grow in Him. He knows where we reside and how we struggle to move on. He knows the inner roots within us which prevent this. He knows our name and every inch of our being. He knows our mother's house.

All those things we hate about ourselves, He knows, and He will not let us go! He is a persistent lover and this song will sow this into our hearts. He fathers us into the great journey of the heart.

> What then shall we say to this? If God is for us, who is against us? He who did not spare his own son but gave him up for us all. Will he not also give us all things with him?
>
> —ROMANS 8:31–32

(See Luke 6:38; John 10:28, 16:23, 17:2, 14:27; 1 Kings 3:5; Psalm 37:4; Isaiah 41:10.)

Song Three

Divine Intimacy

3:6–5:8

*T*HIS IS THE day! Who can discern the love of God fully in a man's heart? And all that it accomplishes in God's glory?

We now find within her a new inner strength; that of inner silence. Silence, not at all related to apathy, disinterest, or personal emptiness as in worthlessness, but a stillness merged into genuine worship, birthed within by His glorious presence. She possesses a listening heart; one that is learning to adore Him. He loves this about her!

The allegations from the dark tents are gone. She is washed clean body, soul, and spirit. She now moves fully into His reign. What is she experiencing? Extravagant heavenly presence! Nothing held back!

Oh, how we long for our hearts to be fully merged into His! It's not noisy in heaven. It's not chaotic! But it's the established reign of a glorious holy God. In His presence we are not enslaved in any way. Enormous freedom of heart and soul is bestowed upon us to finally become all we were created to be—one who glorifies Him! In seeing her we come to know Him.

It is within the beauty of His presence we are transformed into His bride. The dark tents no longer claim ownership. They can't. They were always a mockery of who she was intended to become. When the authentic is present, the counterfeit dies.

Essentially The Song is not directed to the human mind. He's not concerned that we study The Song and come away knowing something more about Him. This book is not simply knowledge to create within us a theological understanding of who we are in Christ. Paul does this so well within his letters to the churches.

No, The Song draws us into intimacy. This book does not require understanding within us. It does open the door to sweet perceptions of Him within our hearts; oftentimes perceptions so deep we are not able to fully express them. We are simply on the journey of knowing Him only as His bride would.

When the fullness of Bridegroom love surrounds you and hangs out with you, how do you describe it? I am not sure we can. A quiet heart is the best way to respond.

We confess with our mouths that we are His but now, within the human heart, it is fully accomplished. He sows a knowledge deep within us of His caresses. We are overwhelmed with a love we have never before experienced. It will quiet the human soul and unleash within us a heart which must have more, then more, and still more. In this intimacy we are revealed in Him. And it's not bad news; no, it's great news!

"What is that coming up from the wilderness, like a column of smoke, perfumed with myrrh and frankincense, with all the fragrant powders of the merchant? Behold, it s the litter of Solomon" (3:6)

Look what's rising up from the landscape of our common lives. Chosen and called out of the wilderness into His high places of worship. The entire heavenly family has gathered for this event. Something wonderful is about to happen!

Within the smoke and fragrant powders, the presence of God is gloriously manifested. All throughout the Old Testament, God's presence with Israel was often defined as fragrant smoke.

Smoke has a way of saturating everything around it; but this is not the smelly stuff which burns our eyes and drives us away. No, this smoke is completely fragrant with the best aromas of heaven and earth. This fragrance captures our attention and draws us wonderfully to Him. His presence now saturates every aspect of this gathering.

> *Lord, I come to you soaked with darkness of heart and soul. And you come to me saturated with saving grace. Thank you for these marvelous truths.*

> To the praise of His glorious grace which he freely bestowed on us in the beloved.
>
> —Ephesians 1:6

(See Ephesians 1:6–7, 2:5, 8, 4:7, 6:24; Deuteronomy 40:37.)

"Behold, it is the litter of Solomon. About it are sixty mighty men of the mighty men of Israel, all girt with swords and expert in war" (3:7–8)

A litter or a palanquin is an ancient vehicle found throughout the historic empires. As a glorious king, Solomon was well acquainted with these vehicles. His were lavish in beauty and comfort.

To the extent that men moved this vehicle, it took on a strong similarity to the ark of the covenant. The ark defined the glorious presence of the living God in Israel; and it was moved from place to place on the shoulders of men. This required the involvement of the human heart to maintain God's presence.

This scripture represents a very large heavenly gathering of not only the entourage of a King and the presence of the living God, but also an enormous armed military ready for battle. The metaphor *sixty* represents a huge number in heavenly terms.

All this is coming up out of the wilderness? Why in the world out of the wilderness? Because that's where His future bride is! Because that's where we live! Where was God's mighty presence manifested to Israel? In the wilderness! The place where we live out our lives, sin against the living God, stumble around, fail, get up, try again, fail again, wander about searching for that alone which the living God will supply. All this defines godless, wilderness living. That's where we live.

At some point in our personal stories, we need to choose Him.

He is completely familiar with our personal wanderings in the journey of life. And in spite of everything, He will choose us as His heavenly bride. This song contains a beautiful story of how far heaven is willing to go to attract our hearts.

> O God, thou art my God, I seek thee; my soul thirsts for thee; my flesh faints for thee, as in a dry and weary land where no water is. So I have looked upon thee in the sanctuary, beholding thy power and glory. Because thy steadfast love is better than life, my lips will praise thee. So I will bless thee as long as I live; I will lift up my hands and call on thy name.
>
> —Psalm 63:1–4

(See Luke 22:19–20, 42–43.)

"All girt with swords and expert in war, each with his sword at his thigh, against the alarms of night" (3:8)

The glorious King of heaven is taking a bride for Himself out of the wilderness. It was a big mistake to take the body of Christ down off the cross, and pierce His side. Every drop of His life was released into the earth as an eternal stain poured out in the wilderness. The dirt and the mud of our existence were saturated with His life.

But He's dead! Just a dead carcass! The body is dead! Bury Him! Close the tomb! Political voices declared a final victory—done, finished!

No! Divine history will have the final word! After the stone is removed, He later ascends into His Father's throne room. Human history is now altered. Every man in every nation will be impacted for eternity.

This King, filled with the Holy Spirit and life, searches us out in the dark places. Please find me! If this reflects my outcry, I then discover He already has.

How saved am I? Is it enough? The very earth I walk on is saturated once and for all, throughout history, with the blood and water of God's Lamb.

> In him we have redemption through his blood, the
> forgiveness of our trespasses, according to the riches of
> his grace which he lavished upon us.
>
> —Ephesians 1:8

"Awake my soul!" The Bridegroom of heaven knows fully well who we are, and precisely where we are. He is coming for us! Though products of the wilderness, how often we feel lonely or abandoned. But a fighting army is present on this glorious occasion for the marriage of heaven and earth. War will break out over this event, so His army is present and ready. The full hatred of the enemy in the wilderness will not have its way.

Awake my soul. He is here, the King of glory.

(See Deuteronomy 32:10–14, 6:6, 8:2–3; Isaiah 35; Psalm 107:36–43.)

"Against the alarms by night" (3:8)

> Who is this King of glory? The Lord of hosts, he is the
> King of glory.
>
> —Psalm 24:10

He comes as a Bridegroom Lover into our world, in the vengeance of our God. This wedding between man and God, in the heart of His soul, literally brings the armies of heaven to earth.

The truth is He will fight for you. He will sacrifice for you, no matter what the cost. The battle between heaven and earth is essentially about us. My personal faith statement needs to develop as I am personally loved and valued by the King of heaven. He has the Father's heart; and He has paid my ransom in full.

He has won me! Not as a follower, because that implies some distance. But the truth is the Bridegroom of my soul travels with the entourage of the fiercest of armies. If the prince of darkness messes with me, he's in deep trouble!

Fill my soul with these precious truths. So many days my faith languishes on the precipice of unbelief, especially about me–about who I am, and who I am not.

(See Psalm 49:5–9; 1 Corinthians 6:20, 7:23; Leviticus 5:18–19; Revelation 21:17.)

"The king made himself a palanquin from the wood of Lebanon" (3:9)

There is no one within our sphere of knowledge or experience like this King. He is not static. He is not simply a theological principle. No, He's vibrant and He is the fullness of His Father's heart. In our day He is the glory within our field of experiential love. He's more alive than anything or anyone else in our universe!

You crave excitement? Crave Jesus! You crave wild love to embrace you? Crave Jesus the King! You crave eternal security? There is no other love on earth offered to you like His. He does not run hot, then cold. And there is no one quite like His bride, birthed within a believer's heart.

He does not want an encounter with you. He wants the knowledge of His love established within your Heart. He wants you!

Knowing you is not a meaningless blitz on this temporal screen of existence. Run after, pursue Him! But the greatest truth is you will find Him seeking after you, and drawing you to Himself.

Are you special? Indeed, you are! If you learn nothing else from this glorious song, then learn this: I am special in His heart. I am special and chosen by Him! And I will continue to say yes to Him throughout my life.

Through heavenly rebirth He created a heart within me completely suitable for His presence. I am truly His because He has done everything to make this a reality within me.

(See Isaiah 60; Psalm 21:6.)

"The king made himself a palanquin from the wood of Lebanon" (3:9)

The King created this structure, or this designated private place, to enjoy with one other. A palanquin is the same as a litter. The space is small and not designed to transport a crowd. It's designed for face-to-face encounters. It's here the heart of the bride is fully birthed.

> And we all, with unveiled face, beholding the glory of the Lord are being changed into his likeness from one degree of glory to another, for this comes from the Lord who is the Spirit.
>
> —2 Corinthians 3:18

How is it that God would begin this book with so outrageous a call upon our lives as to seeking the kisses of His mouth? How is it He has built this private place, never suitable for a crowd, but only for Him and His bride? Unfortunately it is us who brings in the world's clutter surrounding our souls.

These kisses are about Him! They are woven into a deeper revelation of who He is within all that we are. His kisses are filled with overflowing revelation of His personal presence within us, body, soul, and spirit.

> Thou hast said, 'seek ye my face.' My heart says to thee,
> 'Thy face, Lord do I seek.' Hide not thy face from me.
>
> —Psalm 27:8–9

His palanquin represents union in Christ and all the deeper knowledge of the heart, which is authentically produced within His bride. I truly become His workmanship. What I am unable to perform in my relationship in Christ, He performs in me.

So kiss me again, Oh, Lover of my soul.

The apostle Paul says to each of us in 1 Corinthians:

> Do you not know that you are God's temple and that
> God's Spirit dwells in you?
> —1 Corinthians 3:16

My normal response to this word of God has mostly been: "No, I don't have clue!" This word is about "Christist in you, the hope of glory" (Col. 1:27).

(See Hosea 2:16–20, 1 Corinthians 3:16–17; 2 Corinthians 10:4–5; Romans 6:1–11; Psalms 27:8–9, 67:1–2.)

"King Solomon made himself a palanquin from the wood of Lebanon" (3:9)

This famous wood from Lebanon does not decay. Our personal relationship with the King of the human heart also does not decay. It is steeped in His eternal blood. I am never lost, than recovered over and over again. I have been lost, but through my confession of faith and Christ's word on the cross, "it is finished," is eternally stamped on my heart.

> "Know the Lord," for all shall know me, from the least
> of them to the greatest. For I will be merciful toward
> their iniquities, and I will remember their sins no more.
> —Hebrews 8:11–12

(See 2 Corinthians 3:16–18; Isaiah 42:1–5; Hebrews 12:22–24; Jude 24–25; Matthew 21:30–31; John 17.

"He made its posts of silver, its back of gold, its seat of purple; it was lovingly wrought within by the daughters of Jerusalem" (3:10)

This enclosure has a structure of silver which represents redeemed and transformed humanity. Silver has a beautiful surface that reflects all that He is; and this is created within me. This is uniquely established within us an innate part of this great tabernacle of His presence! Amazing!

He creates the palanquin as the place of intimacy, as well as a place of cherished worship in His people. This private place is an image of a redeemed heart which will glorify His Father.

In the very people God lost in the fall of all humanity, He does far more than simply saving us from eternal judgment. He creates within us the heart of His bride. It is within her heart He shares His glory. It's God's plan and image of married love.

> I in them and thou in me, that they may become perfectly one, so the world may know that thou hast sent me and hast loved them even as thou hast loved me. Father, I desire that they also, whom thou hast given me, may be with me where I am, to behold my glory which thou hast given me in thy love for me before the foundation of the world.
>
> —JOHN 17:23–24

Her yes opened the door to the creation of His private throne room. I suspect she, as well as us, didn't begin to understand the glorious miracles appointed to take place within us. We don't begin to perceive the power of His presence and His longing for union in His people.

No more trying to prove to others that I'm genuinely spiritual. It's done! I *am* because He's on the throne in married love. He chose me, and at some point I said yes to this wonderful union.

Within us He will have that place welcoming His fullness and His glory. It will look like a throne. Amazing! Glory to God in the highest! And who we are will naturally reflect His glory. Silver naturally reflects His presence. Amen!

> For we are his workmanship, created in Christ Jesus for good works, which God prepared beforehand, that we should walk in them.
>
> —EPHESIANS 2:10

See John 17:17–26; Psalm 139:7–8; 1 Corinthians 1:28–31; Romans 3:21–26.)

"King Solomon made himself a palanquin" (3:9)

I have been thinking more and more about the divine power of His revelation dwelling within us. My understanding as to how to perceive the language of the Holy Spirit is so limited. I have observed in so many of God's people that Christ has been reduced to ink. The Word of God breathes and actively flows into the heart of His bride. I seldom cherish this phenomenal work He has been performing within me.

Our perceptions of this Bridegroom are not simply cognitive. Revelation not only involves our minds, but more the illumination of our hearts. It is all the result of His life flow revealing His presence into my soul and spirit. It is my heart made alive to live authentically in the truth of His person. When I do this it's never just ink. It's breath!

Created in God's image means we have interior receiving sets built into our hearts. We are able to communicate with Him through the mind of our spirit within His glorious Spirit. In Christ the link up is fully established. But now the discernment and the listening heart needs to function. This is one of the ways we grow into a deeper knowledge of Him. Then basically our emotions will function properly?

Not necessarily! Our discernment of the Bridegroom of the heart will be expressed in many forms. It may, even more, be expressed in our hearts and souls united in His presence, birthing authentic worship within us. I hunger for this flow of revelation!

> ...that the God of our Lord Jesus Christ, the Father of glory, may give you a spirit of wisdom and of revelation, that you may know what is the hope to which he has called you.
>
> —Ephesians 1:17

The palanquin relationship is intensely private. It is not created for the presence of our daily world. It is for private loving with the Savior of our souls. He knows my name as well as my address. It's time we knew His!

> What no eye has seen, nor ear heard, nor the heart of
> man conceived, what God has prepared for those who
> love him. God has revealed to us through the Spirit. For
> the Spirit searches everything, even the depths of God.
>
> —1 Corinthians 2:9–10

(Jude 24; Acts 17:27–28.)

"King Solomon made himself" (3:9)

As I have meditated for years the message of The Song, my understanding of the human heart has completely changed. This scripture describing how the King Himself designed and created this special place within us has expanded my knowledge of the heavenly dynamics which involve us deeply in God's overall plans.

I've come to believe a better visual of the heart is NASA's control center at launch time. A large group of workers oversee every aspect of this procedure using hundreds of computers. The power displayed controls every aspect of this scientific feat; and the world is captivated. Liftoff is achieved and the space shuttle soars into space and disappears from our view. This space appears to us as eternity, which is truly God's world.

The greater dynamic is heaven's control center built within the human heart. Not a center to bring us into subservience, but to make us operational. If anything relates to God's eternal world better than anything else here on earth, it is the human heart. It's not just about liftoff and soaring into heavenly places, but more in sharing His eternal glory. How often He has called her to His high places and will continue to do so.

> The mystery hidden for ages and generations but now
> made manifest to his saints. To them God chose to make
> known how great among the Gentiles are the riches of
> the glory of this mystery, which is Christ in you, the
> hope of glory.
>
> —Colossians 1:26-

It's not so much about the trip, but the relationship. We're not programmed for trips, but for worship equipped in the heart of His bride. And consider the address: living in the center of a magnificent military, saturated in the presence of the living God.

A group of hearts gathers to pray for those in India, Africa, and prisons in Russia, and the dynamic powerful liftoff occurs. God's glory is manifested! The control centers are functional and the shuttle is operational, delivering a revelation of God's great presence.

In the following scriptures in Song Three, an excited Bridegroom describes His bride in totally different terms. She silently stands nearby and, I believe, she is utterly astounded as He describes who she now is. Look at the changes which are emerging within her.

> And we all, with unveiled face, beholding the glory of
> the Lord, are being changed into his likeness from one
> degree of glory to another; for this comes from the Lord
> who is the Spirit.
>
> —2 Corinthians 3:18

(See Revelation 1:10, 4; Psalms 8:3, 21:1–7; 29:1–2; 46:10–11, 72:18–19; John 14:21.)

"Go forth, O daughters of Zion, and behold King Solomon, with the crown with which His mother crowned him on the day of his wedding, on the day of the gladness of his heart" (3:11)

If we authentically connect into the gladness of His heart, our entire personality would radically change. His gladness connects us to the river of joy flowing from His Father's heart. That's life changing! Simply experiencing the power of His joy would impact every inch our beings. We might also enjoy great health!

> Thou dost show me the path of life, in thy presence
> there is fullness of joy, in thy right hand are pleasures
> for evermore.
>
> —Psalm 16:11

(See Isaiah 66:10–14; Luke 6:45; 2 Corinthians 8:1–5, 12:7, 4:15; 1 Timothy 1:12–17.)

"His mother crowned Him on the day of his wedding" (3:11)

His mother is now mentioned, which speaks of His full humanity. Our Savior, our Lover, the Bridegroom of our hearts is fully man and much more. The metaphor *mother* is also associated with the body of believers here on earth. He alludes to this group in 1:8 when He suggests they are a good place to pasture her kids—the body of Christ wearing earthly shoes, as He once did.

> For we have not a high priest who is unable to sympathize with our weaknesses, but one who in every respect has been tempted as we are, yet without sinning. Let us then with confidence draw near to the throne of grace, that we may receive mercy and find grace to help in time of need.
>
> —Hebrews 4:15–16

Heaven now rejoices over His choice of a bride. She is now seen as His crown. One who fully exalts Him! Her move into union in Him will reflect His presence and His glory. She is no longer the woman from the dark tents. Enormous transformation has taken place within her. Her presence is His presence! Her presence glorifies and exalts Him, thus crowning Him! This represents the church.

In this world, this vision should nourish our outlook on life. We often see ourselves as the abandoned lonely Christian. We so easily get lost in this life, which creates a wandering spirit within us. This worn-out vision of life must be handed back to Him as a piece of soiled apparel clothing our hearts.

Praise into worship lifts our hearts by His blood to cleanse and open our eyes to behold Him in His reigning glory. This is the One we praise today!

(See Colossians 3:1–4; Revelation 22:17; Romans 8:18; 1 Peter 1:5–9.)

"On the day of his wedding, on the day of the gladness of his heart" (3:11)

I am invited into the holy of holies by the high priest of my heart. I now enter in, not as the scrubwoman nor am I sent in to dust off the ark of the covenant.

No! The enormous truth about *me* is that I enter as His bride. I am destined to share in His wealth and glory! This very special Bridegroom of my heart and soul has chosen me. He chose me long before I chose Him. He desires to establish within me this quality of union. This is my eternal destiny! He has become my "new and living way."

> God is love, and he who abides in love abides in God,
> and God abides in Him.
>
> —1 John 4:16

(See 1 John 4:13–21; Hebrews 10:20; Ephesians 1:3–14, 2:13; Psalm 89:12–17.)

"Behold you are beautiful, my love, behold you are beautiful" (4:1)

A thrilled Bridegroom is speaking. It's about the marriage of the heart. Throughout life we give ourselves so freely to unsuitable liaisons. Our hungering after authentic love leads us down some dark alleys. But we have His Word concerning who we are.

If you had ever said that Jesus Christ is excited over enjoying a closer relationship with me, my answer would have said, "No way! I'm quite sure I'd drive Him nuts!" It may be that because the range of my feelings concerning *me* run more cold than hot. And I've always projected them into His feelings towards me. I suspect this is why He has pushed me to spend so much time in The Song. There is so much in me He needs to change!

He inspired this song to woo us into marriage love, and to create the Spirit of the bride within us. Now look at this one and who she has become. She entered the wine house in 1:4 and experienced a vibrant breathing person who is the living Savior. And she will discover personally, more and more, that in every way He is the dynamic Bridegroom of life.

Marriage union is a continual rebirth within us to become fully His.

(See Isaiah 61; 1 Corinthians 2:10–16; 2 Corinthians 6:11–13; Ephesians 3:20.)

"My love, behold you are beautiful" (4:1)

> He destined us in love, to be his sons through Jesus
> Christ, according to the purpose of his will, to the praise
> of his glorious grace, which he freely bestowed on us in
> the beloved.
>
> —EPHESIANS 1:5–6

Throughout her life in the dark tents, she had many words spoken over her. "Her mother's sons were angry with her." These words defined the meaning of her life—words which never affirmed her. Words which were defined to keep her lost. Darkness does that.

No longer! He now calls her "my love" and "my bride." His outflow of life is filled with overflowing love. We are not relating to ink, but to breath. His presence creates life out of death! His union with her has created an operational heart.

His search found her! But she was never considered someone of worth—definitely not beautiful. Who could find anything of value in her? Only the wilderness labels people this way.

Watch out for these words: "my love." They are expressed all the way through this song. "My love" is a confession from the heart of God's throne; from the heart of a Father's love.

> The Lord, your God is in your midst, a warrior who
> gives victory; he will rejoice over you with gladness, he
> will renew you in his love; he will exult over you with
> loud singing as on a day of festival.
>
> —ZEPHANIAH 3:17

I decide which words I choose to define who I am. "

Savior of my soul, open the ears of my heart. I want to be made Yours. I want my heart filled with Your words as "My love" Your words within me create a new person. I am beginning not to look at all like that old lady. Thank You for loving me long before I would ever treasure loving You.

(See Luke 4:18–19; 1 Corinthians 2:12–13; Ephesians 1:3–10.)

"You are beautiful" (4:1)

So much of what we pursue in life is utterly worthless. It is that which we run after, with all our hearts, which will fully define who we are. He understands this. He sees that which impacts us and thus transforms us. The imprint of this darkness is not our destiny. He's a jealous Bridegroom for His Father's image to be fully developed within His people. So He pursues us like a column of fragrance or smoke, which attests to the enormous drawing power of His Father's presence.

The Father is here and He calls on my company. Not as one bound in the chains of the wilderness, but as one who is free to run, leap, and dance in His presence. He loves this freedom for His children.

> Thou has multiplied, O Lord my God, thy wondrous deeds and thy thoughts toward us; none can compare with thee. Were I to proclaim and tell of them, they would be more than can be numbered.
>
> —Psalm 40:5

(See Psalm 51:12; John 8:32; Romans 5:15, 6:7, 8:1–7; Hosea 14:4–7; Galatians 5:1.)

"Your eyes are doves behind your veil" (4:1)

She's experienced a miraculous transformation. Don't we all long for this as God's people? She has learned to enter into a time of divine separation with her eyes on Him alone. It seems that when the eyes of the heart are separated unto Him and focused, the ears of our hearts function as well—eyes, as well as ears, experiencing His presence and loving it.

This is a repeat of what He said to her in His chambers, in that her extraordinary beauty is due to dove's eyes. Eyes focused on Him in the power of the Holy Spirit. Eyes which receive divine revelation are dove's eyes. Perhaps the bridal beauty of the heart all begins here. If the Lord repeats Himself, then He needs our attention. Too many of His great truths never take root within us due to a distracted heart.

But now she possesses dove's eyes behind her veil. The intensity of this gift created in her is now different. Veil means power. What she now discerns is gloriously powerful!

(2 Corinthians 3:18; John 17:22; Ephesians 3:19–21, 3–4; Luke 2:20, 33–34; Matthew 21:42; 1 John 1:1; Psalm 40:6.)

"Your hair is like a flock of goats moving down the slopes of Gilead" (4:1)

The goats of mount Gilead are an interesting metaphor of spiritual life. How is the Holy Spirit to enlighten our hearts of His divine truths as well as the substance He has birthed within us?

These goats ascend and descend His mountain, or the high places, in utter ease. She had no interest in the high places in Song Two. Now this journey is performed within the heart of one whose feet stand in the dirt of the daily common chores found here on earth.

The hair of these goats is black and wavy. When they descend mount Gilead, from a distance it looks like a flow of glory. They behave as those who belong there. They have been created to do this by God's enormous grace—and so have we.

We live in the valleys of life, but in total ease we leap into His presence—into His reigning love. In the same powerful grace we descend to minister His life force to a dying world.

(See Revelation 21:9; Jude 24–25; Colossians 1:24–29.)

"Your teeth are like a flock of shorn ewes, that having come up from the washing, all of which bear twins" (4:2)

> Therefore, if anyone is in Christ, he is a new creation;
> the old has passed away, behold the new has come.
> —2 Corinthians 5:17

He has birthed within His bride the ability to receive divine revelation; and to absorb it within her spirit. That which is heavenly is embraced by one on earth. Not every earthling is able to receive this knowledge with understanding. It is framed by the Holy Spirit to be revealed within the human heart reborn in Jesus Christ. The life of the old man is shorn away and the heart is fully exposed to Him and in Him. Hallelujah!

This song has everything to do with the marriage of the heart in Christ. It is a heavenly union, and the song, through poetry, defines what it means to become His new creation. We now have the capacity to receive kingdom revelation.

We are students of the Scripture and live with the eyes and the ears of His bride. We receive His spoken word to the heart in beautiful balance with His written Word. The two agree. If we only possessed His spoken word and nothing else, then we would all be starting new religions strangely focused on us. The blessed balance is the marriage of the two—heart revelation woven together in scriptural revelation.

(See Romans 7:6; 2 Corinthians 5:17; Jeremiah 33:11.)

"Your lips are like a scarlet thread, and your mouth is lovely" (4:3)

Thread binds and connects. Harsh words connect us to shame and weave us into bondage. In life's circumstances we often lose heart. Words can be totally devastating! We often need professional help to disconnect our hearts from desolation and trauma. Words are that powerful! I suspect words have done more damage within us than actual knives and swords.

He loves her words. They are a scarlet thread leading hearts into a relationship full of His life. Scarlet, in that which draws and connects us, is washed in His life blood; redemptive saturated words. It's a thread, and not a rope, drawing us to Him; not for bondage, but for greater freedom and glory.

Our relationship in Him is a combination of this supernatural scarlet thread and a heart centered in Him. He draws us into His life flow as we desire to pursue Him. Both components are necessary, but His scarlet thread or His words of life are full of His glory.

My simple yes to Him are often times in utter weakness. His thread is full of connecting power. My response is focused weakness. What a pair we make—focused weakness connected with enormous heavenly glory!

Her mouth, her heart, her words glorify the fullness of His life. He says, "Your mouth is lovely." Our words of praise and thanksgiving connect us into His life flow.

> My mouth will speak the praise of the LORD, and let all
> flesh bless his holy name"
>
> —PSALM 145:21

(See Psalms 146:1–2; 149; 150.)

"Your cheeks are like halves of pomegranates behind your veil" (4:3)

The vision of her face, kissed many times in His presence, He compares with a half of a pomegranate. If you have ever cut this fruit in half, you will have its interior juices flowing all over you, saturating everything it touches with one of the most powerful dyes in nature. Life saturates us with all kinds of stuff. So how much more it is true of His life flow!

In His intimate presence we are eternally changed. Even her outer countenance wears His presence. All that she is inwardly, as well as outwardly, is eternally transformed in His glorious presence. Everything touched by His flow of life is stained and saturated by His lifeblood.

So now she is perfected? No, as long as she is housed within the formation of the flesh, she will struggle.

His blood was released to completely change me. How much can He really save me? More than I ask or know!

> *I welcome all that you are, to change all that I am. I welcome that your life stains me within.*

(See Exodus 24; Matthew 26:26–28; Hebrews 9:11–14.)

"Your neck is like the tower of David, built for an arsenal, whereon hang a thousand bucklers, all of them shields of warriors" (4:4)

How did a common laborer in the vineyards of this world become like this? She's no different from the rest of us. Or is she? It can be said that her roots are the same as ours.

We have no concept of the power of God we possess on this earth. We are too subjected to the natural weaknesses of the flesh, and our faith focus is consumed by this. It's time to make God's word our focal point over all our interior feelings of inadequacy. He says where two or three are gathered together His power is manifested. It is about *Him*, as well as about us.

She is not governed by a wandering heart or spirit. From the time of her first focus in crying out for His kisses until now, her life has increasingly become focused on Him. The results within her are now supernaturally natural.

David was a warrior king, and when his army was in town, they would store their weapons in the palace towers. They also would hang their shields outside of the tower windows. The sun would reflect off of them and confirm the presence of a mighty army.

He now uses this as a metaphor of her beauty. She was never simply a pretty face. Her countenance displayed the power of heaven's throne room. Her neck turns her head to focus on Him and the Spirit's reflection is dazzling. She now naturally reflects His powerful presence!

(See Job 10:16; Ezekiel 1:4–14; Hosea 5:14, 6:1–3; Revelation 5:5.)

"Your two breasts are like two fawns, twins of a gazelle that feed among the lilies" (4:5)

The gazelle is not only at home on the plains where normal people might live, but in the high places as well. In ease they travel back and forth. They are at home in two worlds.

Christ functioned naturally, then supernaturally, in both worlds. His words filled baskets full of bread and fish. His words filled their hearts to overflowing. The huge gatherings following Him beside the Sea of Galilee would not leave His presence.

A woman's breasts have always been part of her beauty. But they also provide her with the ability to nurture new life. Her role as a mother defines her inner strength, whether she is one by nature, or she is one who meets the needs of those who surround her. A man's breast, as well, provides the enormous strength of commitment for the protection of life.

When we are full of the Holy Spirit, we are full of heaven's life equipping us to nurture. His or her breasts are two wells full of the knowledge of the living God. We are naturally super naturally equipped to glorify Him!

(See John 16:3; Acts 4:8, 9:17; Ephesians 3:19; Mark 3, 14:17; Luke 4:14.)

"Until the day breathes and the shadows flee, I will hide me to the mountains of myrrh and the hill of frankincense" (4:6)

This is a repeated theme as in 2:17. These are rugged mountains full of the treasures of His life and glory. Natural man cannot go in and out in natural strength. A life filled with the Holy Spirit is incited to spend time in the high places. The Holy Spirit just naturally will take us there in praise unto worship and in quiet meditation. Our walk in faith is eloquently defined to draw us closer to Him. It was never intended to simply be ho hum or same old same old.

This hill of frankincense pertains to His relationship with His father, the God of this universe. Frankincense describes the beautiful aroma and His enormous drawing power to the heart and soul. There is no thought here of laboring to get up that mountain. We cannot choose to make it on our own. He takes us there, intimately closer to the living God.

Ascension is now a natural part of her life in Christ. When I offer Him the sacrifice of praise, I am positioning my heart and soul for ascending in His Holy Spirit. My eagle's wings are activated to move into the high places of His divine presence. We ascend and He creates within us the heart of worship.

> He has made my feet like hind's feet, and set me secure
> on the heights.
>
> —Psalm 18:33

> But they who wait for the Lord shall renew their strength,
> they shall mount up with wings like eagles, they shall
> run and not be weary, they shall walk and not faint.
>
> —Isaiah 40:31

Into the place of personal worship, I believe the noise of the world is strongly hindered or perhaps fully hindered. Because they are His high places and they belong to His bride as well.

(See Song of Songs 2:17; Psalms 18:31–36, 27:5, 43:3; Hebrews 8:5–6; Exodus 19:4; Ephesians 2:18–22.)

"You are all fair my love; there is no flaw in you" (4:7)

Be quiet O my soul, and receive His word implanted within me—this word, "my love," which is powerful and commanding within me. His word is vigorous and authoritative!

But for this quality of relationship in Him, I must possess a hearing heart. It has always intrigued me that in the marvelous list of the qualities she possesses, the ear was never mentioned. I have come to believe that all of her beautiful qualities create the hearing heart.

(See Revelation 3:20–22; Matthew 12:42; John 5:30, 10:3.)

"Come with me from Lebanon, my bride; Come with me from Lebanon" (4:8)

In this journey in Song Three she has naturally moved into the position of bride. She did not seek this exalted place, she sought Him. And He supernaturally created this place of intimacy within her. This is the first time in The Song He calls her "My bride."

Lebanon is thought to be a metaphor of a place of seclusion for married love. How often God's Spirit must long for this same time of seclusion within us.

He and his Father wasted no time bringing her into His family as His Son's bride. He'd been waiting a long time, and He still waits for us. But in 3:1 she tells us, "I sought Him whom my soul loves." She continues to awaken within us this same urgency as she says, "I found Him whom my soul loves, I held Him and would not let Him go" (3:4).

She first became His child by receiving His saving grace for sinners. She grew in the great depth of His grace to now be His bride. She pursued Him! The more time she spent in His presence, the more her heart became loosened from other attachments.

This describes her incredible journey. It takes a heart fleeing the dark tents to teach us these things. From the moment she said in 3:2, "I will arise now," she was so occupied with Him that she forgot about herself. In a beautiful unhampered focus she pursued Him.

However, I do believe He never gave up on her. He and His angels were participating in this entire scene. He is intent on calling her "My bride."

> Blessed is he whom thou dost choose and bring near, to dwell in thy courts. We shall be satisfied with the goodness of thy house, thy holy temple.
>
> —PSALM 65:4

His quality of passion is directed to us as well. Why do you think the Father's heart pursued the creation of this love song within a man's heart? To engage all who would desire more of His Bridegroom Son.

Did the living God birth this particular song within Solomon's heart as an inauguration of a deeper relationship with Israel in the building of the first permanent tabernacle for His presence? David longed to build this but God would not allow it. It was to be done through Solomon's hands. We are destined to become the tabernacle.

> But from there you will seek the Lord your God, and
> you will find him, if you search after Him with all your
> heart and with all your soul.
>
> —Deuteronomy 4:9

(See Ezra 8:21; Deuteronomy 4:25–31, 32:12–13; Psalms 9:10, 63:1–4, 119:2; Zephaniah 2:3.)

"Depart from the peak of Amana, from the peak of Senir and Hermon, from the dens of lions, from the mountains of leopards" (4:8)

We are a people who hunger for a spirit world. But this could be a destructive journey for the heart and soul. As long as we reject a Savior's love in the person of Jesus Christ, we remain deceived wanderers.

In the supernatural world in which she is called to now travel and reign in as the King's bride, there are pitfalls. Christ is defined as the lion of Judah. He connects Himself to Israel in the enormous strength of a kingly rein.

But now other lions, as well as leopards are mentioned. The spirit world is His, but at this time in history the other lions and leopards are the destroyers and deceivers of men. They are possibly allowed to exist to offer us a choice. It is important to the Father and the Son that we deliberately choose Him.

Today there are too many spiritual journeys open to us into these high places, or the spirit world. It is a place we are allowed to go because we are created in God's image. But it is a dangerous place to wander into. Even here we are not the masters we perceive we are. Here we are dinner!

As you have come fully into our world, you now draw us again, more fully into your Father's world.

> That the God of our Lord Jesus Christ, the Father of glory, may give you a spirit of wisdom and of revelation in the knowledge of him.
>
> —EPHESIANS 1:17

(See Isaiah 35:8–10; Ezekiel 1; Hosea 5:13–15; 2 Timothy 4:17–18; 1 Peter 5:9; Revelation 5:5; Psalm 91:1.)

"You have ravished my heart, my sister, my bride, you have ravished my heart with one glance of your eyes, with one jewel of your necklace" (4:9)

She's been quietly loving His presence. His enormous beauty is now authentically hers as she quietly stands there. Truly, what has she accomplished so far? Nothing spectacular! She simply absorbs His glory, His personal love. And He says, "You are ravishing, (overjoyed, enthralling, captivating), my heart." His word, His presence transforms me.

He's chosen her to bear His glory. Her response is quietly absorbing His presence and becoming all that she is intended to become.

> The Lord is good to those who wait for him, to the soul that seeks him. It is good that one should wait quietly for the salvation of the Lord.
>
> —LAMENTATIONS 3:25–26.

(See 1 Thessalonians 5:23–24; Psalms 131, 62:1.)

"How sweet is your love, my sister, my bride. How much better is your love than wine, and the fragrance of your oils than any spice" (4:10)

Her opening words to Him were her request for His kisses. She did not mess around! She wanted intimacy with Him and especially His kisses. His kisses filled her life with His wine and with His fragrant oil.

He says, "Your love." My love for Him is now developing more of the same quality of His love for me. It's miraculous! This speaks of not only a transformed life, but a transformed heart. He alone can do this in me.

> Arise, shine; for your light has come, and the glory of the Lord has risen upon you.
>
> —Isaiah 60:1

Somehow He has made His home within my brokenness. Loving has never been my strong suit.

Now truly You are my magnificent inner strength of life.

> *As the Lover of my soul, You continually pressed into me for more, than more, and still more. Many times I so easily let You go. How often my commitment in life is to glorify me; and yet You hang on for the ride. You would not let me go. Your love is tenacious. Oh, thank You for that, great Lover of my soul!*

> I have loved you with an everlasting love; therefore I have continued my faithfulness to you.
>
> —Jeremiah 31:3

(See Genesis 9:12–13; Isaiah 63:7; Psalms 25:6–7, 25:4.)

"How sweet is your love, my sister, my bride" (4:10)

The message from the throne is not so much "Do! Do! Do!" Nor is it "Be! Be! Be!" But rather it is: "You are because I AM."

> Hallelujah. For the Lord our God the almighty reigns. Let us rejoice and exult and give him the glory, for the marriage of the lamb has come, and his bride has made herself ready; it was granted her to be clothed with fine linen, bright and pure" for the fine linen is the righteous deeds of the saints.
>
> —Revelation 19:6–8

"Your lips distill nectar, my bride; honey and
milk are under your tongue; the scent of your
garments is like the scent of Lebanon" (4:11)

She has submerged herself into sweet saving grace. A well of
grace is now established within her family line. Honey, nectar, and
milk are heavenly substances now found within her. Before we are
able to give out words of life, we must receive from Him. His words
are filled with life substance and heavenly knowledge.

Daily our lives are saturated with words, but they are nothing
like His. His words expose me, body, soul, and spirit, to the most
sublime flow of life I can ever know. His words express God's fullness of life directed to me. God says to me in The Song:

> …let me see your face, let me hear your voice, for your
> voice is sweet, and your face is comely.
>
> —SONG OF SONGS 2:14

But we've already looked at this word. This is just repetition. You
bet, and praise God for repetition! You find it all the way through
the Scriptures.

The true substance of my life may be found within my words.
Scripture, His Word, feeds the heart and soul. Worship creates the
passion. There are no other words like His. They transform us and fill
our breasts with life-giving words. His word now calls us "bride."

(See 2 Corinthians 12:9; Matthew 4:4; John 8:31, 12:49–50;
Acts 4:31.)

"A garden locked is my sister, my bride, a
garden locked, a fountain sealed" (4:12)

No more angry complaints about the dark tents and those sons
who gave her grief. Her inner energy of heart and soul are now His.
And this is what He is basically saying. As He has transformed and
saved her, He is now capable of saving her family line as well. In our
relationship in Him, our roots of salvation are established not only
to bless my soul, but nations as well.

Sow within me a heart which adores You, as You adore me. I know You are waiting for this quality of faith to be manifested within me. Dig, sow, plant, and fill within me that quality of revelation and knowledge which only intimacy produces. I welcome your presence in all that I am. Thank you for desiring me. This is a one great miracle!

(See Matthew 4:10; John 4:20–24; Philippians 3:3; Revelation 4:14.)

"A garden locked is my sister, my bride" (4:12)

The great banner placed over each of us is the banner of God's love seeking to cover us and draw us deeply within His presence alone. He hungers for focused worship!

We give the fertile soil of worshiping hearts only to glorify Him. We are careful not to plant those showy crops that glorify us. No, we allow Him to plant the ingredients for the tabernacle anointing oil. It is no longer about a heart pursuing Him. He now describes for us a heart established in Him, or a fully operational heart. Wow!

I have always given You my prayer list asking You for many things. This is a privilege You extend to your children. You say, "Ask and you shall receive." But I am now sensing a stronger desire in Your heart: that I would focus on seeking You first and releasing all that I am into Your presence. It's as though I am learning to lean.

> Glory in his holy name; let the hearts of those who seek the Lord rejoice. Seek the Lord and his strength, seek his presence continually.
>
> —1 Chronicles 16:10–11

(See John 20:15; Numbers 24:1–6; Proverbs 4:23.)

*"Your shoots are an orchard of pomegranates
with all choicest fruits, henna with nard,
nard with saffron, calamus and cinnamon,
with all the trees of frankincense, myrrh and
aloes, with all the chief spices"* **(4:13–14)**

He's had His way with her—an expression loaded with negative connotations in our culture. But in this instance the results are glorious! Few have experienced this quality of His loving power.

It seems in Song Three she's just standing around. She's not doing anything spectacular. She's simply absorbing Him. Oh, people of God, let's do the same! Let's learn to stand around silent in His glorious presence. This is a quality of life we seldom testify of.

We face ongoing problems in our journey of life and faith. We don't truly know much about Him personally, especially His presence at home within us. We seem to stay focused on the Christ manifested outside of us. As long as He remains essentially ink and not breath, He is not treasured.

Jesus, the Lover of our souls, as well as the master gardener of our interior lives, sees the wonderful potential of growth within us; growth which glorifies His presence, and sows the seeds of beauty and righteousness. His word sows life seeds, faith seeds, and the seeds of His presence.

Spending a number of years on the mission field does not attest to this production within me. In fact, it was there He confronted me with an astounding word. He said to me, "I don't love you for what you do. I love you, and I want you." I thought He had me because I was a missionary. Apparently not! It was then, nearly forty years ago, that my journey in The Song began.

> Christ in you, the hope of glory.
>
> —Colossians 1:27

This is His word and His idea of planting His Spirit richly into the souls of men. He doesn't demand gardens within us. His presence simply creates them to glorify His Father.

For as the earth brings forth its shoots, and as a garden causes what is sown in it to spring up, so the Lord God will cause righteousness and praise to spring forth before all the nations.

—Isaiah 61:11

Now birth within us eyes that see and ears that perceive Your glorious presence. Help us to not only acknowledge Your presence but also perceive who You are as the master gardener. Plant everything necessary to glorify Your Father on high.

(See John 4:7–42; 2 Corinthians 2:14.)

"Nard and saffron, calamus and cinnamon, with all the trees of frankincense, myrrh, and aloes, with all the chief spices" (4:14)

His life is the substance of good seed. In our daily lives we put beauty on, but only on the outside. Applying good make-up is an art as well as a multimillion-dollar industry. Make-up creates false beauty. But so what! Just as long we find something to improve our desirability.

The Song now shows us He possesses all the seed required to authentically birth within us genuine, eternal beauty that glorifies the Father. This impossible work is essentially His work manifested within us. Scripture, praise, worship, and fellowship are the seeds we receive into our hearts—seeds full of His presence and glory.

(See Ephesians 2:10; Psalms 3:3, 8:3–6, 26:6–8; Psalm 63; Hosea 14:6–7; John 12:3.)

"A garden fountain, a well of living water, and flowing streams from Lebanon" (4:15)

He's created within her a dynamic outflow of life as she worships. His presence creates wells of living water.

In Song Two she did not possess this perception of herself. She was on a reckless journey which allowed her to make a careless decision in her spiritual life.

Now He has created within her a well of living water. Not stagnant in any way. Religious form can become stagnant over the years. No, this is a dynamic flow of life within her heart. Amen.

She dug this well and filled it with so much diligence. No. He loved on her and His beautiful presence is the well. Along the journey she agreed and accepted this revelation of Him as the Lover of her soul.

Full wells naturally overflow. Don't we long for this as His people? Don't we hunger for this natural manifestation in faith to reveal itself within all that we are? This is what The Song is meant to teach us. Our hearts are a treasure house and He is the treasure.

He naturally overflows as He did in John 4 into that pathetic woman at the well, whose life was utterly empty and wasted.

> Blessed be the God and Father of our Lord Jesus Christ,
> who has blessed us in Christ with every spiritual blessing
> in the heavenly places.
>
> —Ephesians 1:3

And in Song Three this is exactly where she has been—not an out of body experience, but in heart fullness He alone provides. Jesus: full of grace and truth, full of His Father's glory, fullness of joy, and this list continues on.

(See John 2:7–10, 4:7–15; Ephesians 5:26; Psalms 16:11, 36:7–8.)

"Awake, O north wind, and come, O south wind. Blow upon my garden" (4:16)

She now takes personal ownership as in "my garden." This is about His loving me. She is now saying, "Look fully at me, and learn of Him. His presence naturally flows within me."

She may not be naturally beautiful as one confined to the fields of Kedar. But the great truth now is that she is supernaturally beautiful. She now naturally reflects all that He is. She's not squeezing out any effort to look spiritual. She is simply at rest in receiving His personal love for her.

Revelation not only provides us with coherent thinking. But revelation will reveal authentic life and glory—His! How would it ever be possible to bundle up all of this into some comprehensive principle? A principle cannot pull this off, but a living, breathing Savior can.

Our hearts now eternally rest because of who it is at home within us—full force revelation presence, glory and power: His!

"Quiet, O my soul. The Lord of glory is digging, planting, and cultivating my heart and soul, to not only know Him intimately, but to truly glorify Him. It is His work, His power, His substance, and His fullness of life, and yet perfected within me. In the presence of the Lord there is great joy and we become like Him." She was created by the heart of God to teach us this.

> O continue thy steadfast love to those who know Thee,
> and thy salvation to the upright of heart.
>
> —Psalm 36:10

> Thou openest thy hand, thou satisfiest the desire of every
> living thing.
>
> —Psalm 145:16

(See Colossians 1:24–29; Ephesians 2:2, 22, 3:14–21; Psalms 4:3, 25:4, 91:14–16; 2 Corinthians 4:16–18.)

"Let its fragrance be wafted abroad. Let my beloved come to his garden and eat its choicest fruits" (4:16)

The confession of her life is all about His presence. "Enjoy Me." She is internally focused on Him. Personal faith is her response to all that He has created within her person. She's saying, "Be glorified in me."

If you examine her carefully throughout Song Three, she has done nothing to deserve heaven's attention. Throughout The Song she just quietly hangs around. Yes, choosing to spend time in His presence, her interior composure is focused on Him. She's not telling

Him all her troubles and immediate needs. No, she's quietly focused on Him.

> For the Lord is righteous, he loves righteous deeds; the upright shall behold his face.
>
> —PSALM 11:7

What is she receiving from Him? He deserves my time alone in Him; receiving His Bridegroom perceptions as to how He delights in me: as to how He values who I am, as to how He adores my time and presence freely given to Him.

Blow you winds of heaven and earth and let us inhale His glory.

> *Come over and over again and abide in me as Your garden of life. Be reverenced there! Be fulfilled there! Continue to make it a place where You belong, O Lover of my soul. There is no one like You. Create within me a flow of the aroma of heaven, as You did within her. Fill my daily circumstances with the aroma of Your presence.*

Is this too sappy? Often I have thought so. It's not a respectable prayer I would pray at the weekly Bible study. No, not at all! But I sense He may be saying this. He is not maudlin. He is eternally deep and gloriously in love with His people. Unfortunately, this is a revelation that continues to escape His people. So, it's fine to get sappy and syrupy once in awhile.

> The disciple Peter answered him, 'Lord, to whom shall we go? You have the words of eternal life; and we have believed and have come to know, that you are the Holy One of God.
>
> —JOHN 6:67–79

> *Lord, to whom else can we go? Who creates within us lush gardens out of utter desolation? Lord to whom else can we go?*

(See Isaiah 2:3; Jeremiah 1:11–12; Colossians 3:16; Psalms 119:129–130, 145:16; Isaiah 60:1.)

*"Let my beloved come to his garden,
and eat the choicest fruits" (4:16)*

It's about married love, especially with Him, the Savior of our souls. His heart is fully involved first with His Father and subsequently in us.

Your feelings towards Jesus and towards others into which you have entered into marriage intimacy, may be dead. Now is the time to move quietly into His fullness of life, which is known to raise the dead!

(Study Lazarus in John 11 and John 15:4–5.)

*"I come to my garden, my sister, my bride, I gather
my myrrh with my spice, I eat my honeycomb with
my honey, I drink my wine with my milk" (5:1)*

OK, let's get real! How does the living God truly feel about me? Such doubts maintain our proneness to wonder. He loved me yesterday, but does He really like me today? I am not consistent, so why would I believe He is?

This is it: He's wildly in love with me! All day long He pursues me as a lover! He can't get enough of me! I am one of His favorites—as you are.

He truly welcomes us with kissing love. His kisses, within your hearts, produce vital revelation of His quality of life. He is the lover appointed to our journey here on earth. He chose us for bridal intimacy. He won't let us go! We are His favorites, and is this platitudinous? Not on your life!

> …rather speaking the truth in love, we are to grow up
> in every way into Him who is the head, into Christ.
> —Ephesians 4:15

(See John 15:7–11; Psalm 105:4.)

"Eat, O friends, and drink: drink deeply, O lovers" (5:1)

She has become a credible source of His life flow. His life births life. Sin births death. His life creates glorious life! However, her desire for Him placed her within this dynamic flow of revelation coming through Him from His Father's heart.

Even lost, we are never that far from Him. At some point she focused on Him from the fields of life and sought His redemptive love.

To move on more deeply there needed to be a successive yes on her part. She traveled in Him very imperfectly, but her perfection and inner strength was always to be found in Him. In a resting soul she has become authentically His. She never deserved this, nor earned it. Her heart simply said, "Draw me!"

(See Acts 7:49–50; Psalm 16; Colossians 2:10; John 10:10.)

"I slept, but my heart was awake. Hark. My beloved is knocking, 'open to me, my sister, my love, my dove, my perfect one; for my head is wet with dew, my locks with the drops of night'" (5:2)

Now the eternal conflict, the daily wrestling match. How can this fusion of heaven and earth really work? On earth, in the context of daily living, we ask, "Can this marriage work?"

The scene in this song now radically changes. But the words and the teaching are the foundation for where we now live. She is firmly His bride, and she is committed to this relationship. But this now has to do with her personal time to sleep. He neither sleeps nor slumbers. But as a member of the human race, sleep is a justified need.

This scripture teaches us a wonderful truth within His Bridegroom reign. He is also Lord of our nights and our sleep.

> I bless the Lord who gives me counsel; in the night also
> my heart instructs me.
>
> —PSALM 16:7

This is great news because most of us never experience His presence in our sleep. He freely communes with our hearts because they are His. But the downside is that within our conscience we encase everything that has ever happened to us, both good and bad. Those dark fields of Kedar still live there. Within the depths of her being, the dark tents still influence her inner life. The great news is that He is Lord of all that we are! He is there as well! And He is Lord!

> It was a night of watching by the Lord, to bring them out of the land of Egypt.
>
> —EXODUS 12:42

(See Psalms 119:62, 19:1–4, 30:5; Exodus 12:42; Job 35:10.)

"Open to me, my sister, my love, my dove, my perfect one; for my head is wet with dew, my locks with the drops of the night" (5:2)

The love of the Father has sent Him to us not only to be our personal Savior but to become far more within us. All night long He knows we belong to Him. So He takes liberties. He is the Bridegroom and He will behave this way.

> The Lord's portion is his people, Jacob his allotted heritage.
>
> —DEUTERONOMY 32:9

Jesus comes to us in heaven's fullness.

> Full of grace and truth.
>
> —JOHN 1:14

> ...and to know the love of Christ which surpasses knowledge, that you may be filled with all the fullness of God.
>
> —EPHESIANS 3:19

> Which is His body, the fullness of him who fills all in all.
>
> —EPHESIANS 1:23

His countenance drips with glory, and He desires time with her, even in her nights. I personally find this great truth comforting. So often the conflicts, anxieties, and the hostilities of our day create restless nights of conflict and worry. Subsequently, who then controls the heart?

"I had put off my garment, how can I put it on? I had bathed my feet, how could I soil them?" (5:3)

Oops! We saw this coming. A real mismatch! This union is flawed! She wears sandals just like us, as well as just like Him.

He comes in flesh and blood. He altogether understands flesh and blood. He and His Father have done all to bring us into His fullness—something flesh and blood could never merit, nor ever be entitled to.

But have they done enough? Let this giant YES melt away for all eternity the walls of unbelief and complacency.

You have never aborted us. But have we been worth saving?

We have our agendas, as well as our priorities, by which we live. Our lifestyles will not quickly change within us.

You said You stand at the door and knock to enter into sublime fellowship with us. But Lord, sometimes that door is locked!

He will come and awaken our spirits, even if our flesh is contrary. Awake or asleep I am His bride, and He will take liberties within me. Amen!

Many Psalms end with the word *selah*, which can be translated "hooray." I say hooray to this truth! His bridal lordship is over everything recorded within my heart and soul. He now enters my history. Hooray!

> He chose our heritage for us, the pride of Jacob whom he loves. Selah.
>
> —Psalm 47:4

(See Mark 1:1–8; Ezekiel 2:1–2, 43:6–7; Psalm 17:5–8; Proverbs 4:16, 5:1–6.)

"My beloved put his hand to the latch, and my heart was thrilled within me" (5:4)

This Bridegroom doesn't know His boundaries. He crosses all of them with ease. Amen and hooray!

Who is this that reaches into her heart and unlatches the door? He shows freedom in this relationship within her. The latch of her heart appears to be only on the inside. It is not available to the public, unless she throws opens the door. No, her heart is His and He has this freedom.

Where did all this take place? In the palanquin, in the garden within her established by Him, and in the high places of worship. He's free to take liberties as Bridegrooms do.

Essentially what is this about?

> Christ in you, the hope of glory.
>
> —Colossians 1:27

Christ in you, the bride from the tribe of humans, as well as the worst of humans, the family tribe of Kedar. Her feet were filthy from mandated work in those fields of life. We all approach Him with dirty feet from the places we freely connected to. Also those places we were forced to live in. We travel in life in the defilement of heart and soul, thus filthy feet.

She seemed to first seek Him out. But she found, in the strong arms of heaven, the Godhead fully seeking her out in the fullness of heaven's joy. Her presence now completes heaven's joy.

(See Genesis 25:12; 1 Chronicles 1:29; Psalm 120:5; Song of Songs 2:6; Isaiah 21:16–17, 60:1–7; Jeremiah 9:13; Ezekiel 27:21.)

"I arose to open to my beloved, and my hands dripped with myrrh, my fingers with liquid myrrh, upon the handles of the bolt" (5:5)

Who is this that freely opens the latch to our hearts and leaves us so full of the anointing of the Holy Spirit? The Lover of our souls? Yes! The glorified King of all of life? Yes! And still far more! He moves more deeply within all that we are and leaves us with enormous grace and spiritual anointing, thus His kisses.

Dripping with myrrh defines an anointing of the Holy Spirit. Myrrh was especially present in the holy place as well as in the holy of holies. Myrrh awakens us to the presence of the living God. Perhaps in natural strength she was unable to open the door. Even in enormous weakness the gift of God and the strength of God are freely given.

He visits us in our nights. Nothing within the darkness of our souls is hidden from His light. All the residue of our falleness is His as well. Selah, hooray! We need to grow in the understanding of the journey of the heart as to who He is within the structure of who we are. Nothing is hidden! Hooray and selah!

(See Psalms 51:11–12, 23:3; Isaiah 58:10–12.)

"I sought him, but I found him nought; I called him, but he gave no answer" (5:6)

After all, she's not that different from you and me. She possesses a human heart no different from ours. He's ditched her! We knew this couldn't last!

> By day the Lord commands his steadfast love; and at
> night his song is with me, a prayer to the God of my life.
> —PSALM 42:8

I do appreciate the Lord has written into The Song a person very much like ourselves. All day long our hearts fail Him many times over. His word shows us an honest journey of the heart of flesh. There is nothing superficial taking place here. He disturbed her personal agenda. He seems to act as though He has this right. He does!

But she opened the door and He is gone. The liquid myrrh, now what is it for? He's gone! God appoints unto this heart a time of searching. These are not futile useless experiences. They strengthen the resolve of the heart.

This time the apparent absence of His beautiful presence will usher her into a far deeper relationship in Him. Out she goes in panic! But the fields He has established within her will direct her search. She is not lost!

> *Amen! Selah! Hooray! I invite you to more and more take liberties within me. Saturate me with your Bridegroom love!*

> Cast me not away from thy presence, and take not thy Holy Spirit from me. Restore to me the joy of thy salvation, and uphold me with a willing spirit.
> —PSALM 51:11–12

(See Daniel 6:25–28; Psalms 78:8, 37:7; 1 Corinthians 15:58; Hebrews 13:14–15, 6:17–20.)

"The watchmen found me, as they went about in the city; they beat me, they wounded me, they took away my mantle those watchmen of the walls" (5:7)

They are the watchmen of a hostile world. They assault her in order to rob her of His graces. They are hostile to the deeper revelation of His presence within her heart. "Who in the world do you think you are? Someone special? Filled with the Spirit of God? Phooey! You're no different from the rest of us living in the spirit of this world!"

These watchmen are the hostile forces of our world. The last mental activity before sleep energizes these feelings into subconscious action. Give Him conscious praise and worship before slipping into sleep.

More of Him requires more of her. He will love her into wholeness even in the darkest areas of her being. Even there she is His. She is His bride, and at the same time she struggles with the flesh.

So He takes off! This mismatch is now about her heart seriously pursuing Him.

(See Psalms 127:1–2, 3:5, 40:16–17; Jeremiah 31:23–26.)

"I adjure you, O daughters of Jerusalem,
if you find my beloved, that you tell
him I am sick with love" (5:8)

Revelation is not simply being exposed to knowledge. The Song speaks to us, body, soul, and spirit. We are not called to precepts alone, but to a relationship with One who is glorious beyond our imaginations. The apostle John describes Him for us in the first chapter of Revelation.

This is an outcry of her soul for more. She is found wanting, as so are we. But this is a manageable crisis. It's one He allows. When He called her forth to pursue Him, her feet were clean and this created a personal problem to her. It was inconvenient, and it represents the many little things we allow to disturb the journey.

He's withdrawn for a season, and she is struggling. Everything was perfect, and now it's all lost! Not at all! Times of searching Him out when His discernable presence is gone are seasons of a deeper work of the cross.

> When my spirit is faint, thou knowest my way.
>
> —Psalm 142:2

It's no longer about the spirit of the dark tents, but more about the innocent little things of life which distract us. Forget the clean feet, and come away. Reset your priorities.

> The Lord is my chosen portion and my cup; thou holdest my lot. The lines have fallen for me in pleasant places; yea, I have a goodly heritage.
>
> —Psalm 16:5–6

(See Psalms 81:5–16, 84:2; 1 Chronicles 16:11; 1 Peter 5:7; 2 Corinthians 5:6–9.)

"What is your beloved more than another beloved, O fairest among women? What is your beloved more than another beloved, that you thus adjure us?" (5:9)

"O heart of mine, let's have an honest talk. So why is He so special? You've gotten yourself involved in a very demanding relationship. Is He that important?"

These thoughts assail us all the time. Life comes at us, and some of it is pure nonsense and trash. But also much of it is utterly desirable. We face this all the time as we seek to journey with Him in feet of flesh, which need constant cleaning.

> *Savior and Lover of my soul, please create within me authentic love for You and the Father. Create polished gold in the center of my being, which fully reflects You and Your glory. You know how easily distracted I am, and only You can perform this within me.*
>
> *But You know me fully. You know who I am and where I live. And yet Your tenacious love refuses to let me go.*

He'll draw her to himself in many ways. He desires to be fully known by the human heart. We normally desire a more casual relationship. "

Ditch that! Change me, and love me fully!

> In the journey it comes down to this. I sought Thee from a distance and did not know thou was here.[1]
>
> —Saint Augustine

> Return, O my soul, to your rest; for the Lord has dealt bountifully with you.
>
> —Psalm 116:7

(See Hebrews 4:1, 4:10; 2 Corinthians 12:9; Psalms 55:6, 84:2; Habakkuk 2:14; Acts 2:28.)

Song Four

Power and Glory

5:9–8:4

You created the love song of the ages. You caress the human heart into wanting more of You. You truly are the master of the heart, knowing full well how it works. You loosen our bonds to hunger for eternal life. I am not always to suffer want, but to be gloriously fulfilled on Your terms. You are not a meager provider. You love filling to over-flowing. This is Your style.

> You shall no more be termed Forsaken, and your land shall no more be desolate; but you shall be called my delight is in her, and your land married; for the Lord delights in you, and your land shall be married.
>
> —ISAIAH 62:4

We do not have the words to describe all that You are. Please birth the faith to believe about ourselves all that You desire to create within us while in our world. But as one created for Your world, we are the stage and You are on center stage.

Wow, what a show! But it's not a show. It is the genuine fullness of His presence within us, and now His kisses are most appropriate.

You bathed that soul, a product of the dark tents, in a husband's love, and she is radically changed.

You created her to open the door birthing Your intimacy within us. It is Your initiative from the cross unto a marriage union to substantiate the fullness of Your life in us. You fill our tents, our souls, with the sublime beauty of the Father's Heart. You draw us so far beyond our natural parameters. You are the appointed Lover of our souls.

He says, "Listen carefully, and I will not only show and teach you of My transforming love, but I will also tell you how much you thrill Me!"

> Behold, a virgin shall conceive and bear a son, and his name shall be called Emmanuel.
> —Matthew 1:23

God with us, so close to us! The distance He has appointed for our lives births intimacy; the union of hearts becomes a reality. His glory becomes our glory! This is His plan for His people as His bride, and all this thrills the heart of the heavenly Bridegroom. His presence, His glory, His strength creates the heart of the bride within each of us. It is first about *Him* and then wonderfully about us.

"What is your beloved more than another beloved, O fairest among women? What is your beloved more than another beloved, that you thus adjure us?" (5:9)

Oh, come on! Is His love better than all the others? He couldn't be that good! It's just religion.

Not on your life! He's a living breathing person who loves revealing Himself within us.

You have never experienced love until you've known His. He *is* that good! His love is eternal and will search you out until His love for you alone is fulfilled. He *is* that good! In the sphere of loving, He is exceptional! His love alone satisfies the human heart. He truly *is* that good! In fact, He is extraordinary!

How blind, how deaf, and how dumb we are as creatures made

in His image. We are clueless to the fact that the Lover of all eternity seeks to make Himself known personally within each of us. Not to preach at us. Not to condemn us. But to love us, body, soul, and spirit in the depths of heaven's passion.

The last part of Song Three finds her again frantically searching, and she does not find him. She loses her composure. The beautiful, anchored woman of this song has vanished. Her flesh life now seeks Him in the wrong places, and she has not found Him. The ongoing relationship in Him was never fully on her terms.

His great desire is to saturate us with the Bridegroom knowledge of who He is. It is a deeply personal love encompassing both the new woman, as well as the old frantic one. However the old woman of the flesh is withering.

His relationship with her has not been in vain for now she answers her own question to those who are examining her. And life will always challenge us concerning our faith.

She answers with a vivid, living revelation birthed within her, an eternal treasure within her heart. She answers as one who knows Him intimately. So many things within her have gloriously changed.

> He put a new song in my mouth, a song of praise to our God. Many will see and fear, and put their trust in the Lord.
>
> —Psalm 40:3

Again she connects in Him. The quiet one of Song Three now bonds with all that He has established in her. Nothing was lost. His work is solid and trustworthy. But at times outside forces will still confuse and spiritually disorient us.

When I reconnect with my flesh life, I seem to lose the equilibrium He birthed within my spirit. But I have not lost Him. I have not lost anything He has created within me. But if the old lady is in panic, then her noise creates static and then I do lose focus.

But we are blessed for she now possesses a deep clarity by the power of the Holy Spirit. This revelation of the personal Lover of her soul is dynamic and this is what He is now doing within His bride—creating an interior heart and soul knowledge of who He is.

Her heart is beginning to be operational. Selah and hooray!

> All the paths of the Lord are steadfast love and faithfulness, for those who keep his covenant and his testimonies.
>
> —Psalm 25:10

"My beloved is all radiant and ruddy, distinguished among ten thousand" (5:10).

"His head is the finest gold; his locks are wavy, black as a raven" (5:11).

"His eyes are like doves beside springs of water, bathed in milk, fitly set" (5:12).

"His cheeks are like beds of spices, yielding fragrance. His lips are lilies, distilling liquid myrrh" (5:13).

"His arms are rounded gold, set with jewels, His body is ivory work, encrusted with sapphires" (5:14).

"His legs are alabaster columns, set upon bases of gold. His appearance is like Lebanon, choice as the cedars" (5:15).

"His speech is most sweet, and he is altogether desirable. This is my beloved and this is my friend, O daughters of Jerusalem" (5:16).

Revelation is flowing from Your persona, exalted and glorious. You are no longer on the cross of our redemption. You have saved us, and You now draw us out of the dimness of our souls into the radiance of Your glory. This revelation seeded within us, births the bride. All that You are creates the bride. Hallelujah!

The breadth of His reign is universal. His Father will one day be fully known to the entire world He has created. Through her words in 5:16, she brings the universal reigning God infinitely close. In spite of His great glory, or perhaps because of it, she tells us His words are sweet and desirable. They are heavenly honey to the human heart.

> *Please stop my frantic search for this treasure in all the wrong places. Your honey nourishes my inner life. You belong that close to me. I am Yours.*

(See Psalm 116; 1 Corinthians 1:4–9; 2 Corinthians 5:17–20; Luke 2:32.)

"Whither has your beloved gone, O fairest among women? Whither has your beloved turned, that we may seek him with you?" (6:1)

He may be in plain sight. But if the eyes of our hearts are not at all focused, we'll probably miss Him. When she was challenged by the daughters to declare His glorious presence, she answered in the power of the Holy Spirit (5:9, 6:1)

The crowd says, "Where is He, that we may seek Him too?" She is the appointed one to lead this group. She, too, was on the same journey. But as she possessed liquid myrrh in opening her heart more fully to Him in 5:5, this same fragrance is drawing the crowd to Him.

As her journey is just beginning, so is theirs. The search is on!

> Again, the kingdom of heaven is like a merchant in search of fine pearls. Who, on finding one pearl of great value, went and sold all that he had and bought it.
> —MATTHEW 13:45–46

Whose heart is Jesus talking about? His Father's or ours? It's Him who has purchased our heart and soul for a very great price!

(See Luke 11:9–13; Philippians 3:13.)

"This is my beloved, and this is my friend" (5:16)

> *Desiring me, wanting me, with all of your heart, yearning for me? Waiting over the years for me to just a little bit,*

desire You? You wait in the fullness of love to get our attention, and then hopefully capture our hearts.

Thank You for hungering for me. On that special day I finally turn to You and say, "Kiss me," become very special in my heart. "Your name is oil poured out." As one who is seeking You, You create in me a functioning temple of the Holy Spirit.

> Now the Lord is the Spirit, and where the Spirit of the Lord is, there is freedom. And we all with unveiled face, beholding the glory of the Lord, are being changed into His likeness from one degree of glory to another; for this comes from the Lord who is the Spirit.
>
> —2 Corinthians 3:17–8

"Wither has your beloved turned, that we may seek him with you?" (6:1)

We are dealing with a person overflowing with vibrant life, not simply a set of ideas. His presence or His fullness of truth is revelation appointed for sweet encounters. The human mind cannot package these up neatly into religious doctrine. We certainly learn from doctrine, but it's tough to have an intimate relationship with dogma alone.

He's a flowing life force that enters into the deepest and sometimes darkest domain of our beings. He's not afraid of dark places. He's most definitely the light of the world, which is His vibrant divine presence.

> The Lord is my portion," says my soul, "therefore I will hope in him.
>
> —Lamentations 3:2

(See Matthew 4:16, 6:22–23; Luke 1:79, 2:32, 11:35–36; 2 Corinthians 4:6; Lamentations 3:22–26.)

"My beloved has gone down to his garden, to the beds of spices" (6:2)

God delivered and led His people out of Egypt, which represented a life enslaved in the darkness and cruelty of sin. He delivered them miracle by miracle. His hunger was for a people called by His name. He still hungers!

In her frantic search she has asked the daughters as to where He was. They didn't have a clue! Most of us live out our daily lives knowing very little about Him. But as she was asking, she was answering. Her heart was directing her.

Jesus and His Father love to garden; to sow abundant life into their people, to share in them not only the knowledge we desperately need, but the glory as well. I believe they love this garden. I know they deeply love us.

This is a truth worth hanging on to. Right now He is working in His garden sowing a bed of spices. Spices enrich the image of God within each of us by the power of the anointing of the Holy Spirit. It is a shame we know so little about the Holy Spirit. He is so good at His work, and yet we seldom trust in Him.

I am a garden in process. He plants within me revelation upon revelation of His presence and glory. It is true that it is not about me. It is about *Him*, and thus it becomes about me.

> I came that they may have life, and have it abundantly.
>
> —John 10:10

(See Exodus 25:2, 8, 22, 29:45, 30:22–25; Ephesians 2:8–10; 1 Thessalonians 5: 23.)

"To pasture his flock in the gardens and to gather lilies" (6:2)

Where does He hang out with His flock? In His gardens, within the lives of His people who cultivate His presence.

> *Imprint this wonderful truth in my mind, that today You are hanging out with me. Must I seek a great distance to find you? No, just simply quiet the noise within.*

He is the master gardener and this metaphor is used often. His presence and His fullness of life produce seed life within His people. Those who praise unto worship are into garden cultivation. Worship in His presence is never simply a good time or beautiful music. It is time spent in His glory, and this produces an enormous fragrance, which draws the human heart to Himself. He knows what He's doing!

> May the God of peace himself sanctify you wholly; and may your spirit and soul and body be kept sound and blameless at the coming of our Lord Jesus Christ. He who calls you is faithful, and He will do it.
>
> —1 Thessalonians 5:23–24

(See Acts 15:16–18; Psalm 133; Matthew 6:28; Hosea 4:4–9; John 15:5.)

"I am my beloved's and my beloved is mine; he pastures his flock among the lilies" (6:3)

She freely uses the words "my beloved." It is time I do the same. If in my personal prayer times I would approach the living God in the same way, it would thrill His heart and deepen His work within me.

Oh, church, awaken and express yourself in the same manner! Express faith in Him. Through your words bring Him kissing close.

"My beloved" is the intimacy we hungered for in asking for His kisses, which, after all, started this journey. "My beloved" is also a confession of faith out of my mouth. It is a confession He not only loves to hear, but I need to hear as well. "My beloved" produces intimacy.

But is it authentic? I am a wanderer and He knows this about me. Then do I dare say this? Yes, because the seeds of authentic life come from Him. My faithfulness and all my strength are always found within Him, the Savior and Lover of my soul.

> *You are my beloved, not because I have made you this way, but because You have chosen to be this in me. You have*

chosen me to be Your bride. And, Lord, I say yes! Oh, beloved of my soul!

All this creates the stature of a lily within me. A lily is quiet and looks up. It receives the revelation of His presence. It easily receives heaven's dew. A lily knows how to stay quietly connected. Hallelujah!

(See Isaiah 2:3.)

"You are beautiful as Tirzah, my love, comely as Jerusalem, terrible as an army with banners" (6:4)

When she is on the scene, so is His army. And this army displays heaven's banners; more outrageous knowledge and revelation, extravagant and preposterous. She is not simply a pretty face, and He is not simply a religious icon.

Tirzah was a beautiful dwelling place here on earth. It was the area in which royalty loved to establish their homes—perhaps something like Beverly Hills in southern California. All the dwelling places are exceptionally fine. He is now describing her as an exceptionally fine dwelling place—nothing in common with the dark tents of Kedar.

In this case a beautiful heart creates an extraordinary dwelling place. We will know Him in a greater sense and presence than we have ever known Him before. He will be glorified as He has never been before, as more of His people become His functioning bride. She will put on quite a show! No, she will simply be herself.

> Blessed be the Lord, my rock, who trains my hands for war, and my fingers for battle.
>
> —PSALM 144:1

(See John 17; Exodus 17:14; Psalm 29:6; Isaiah 42:10–17.)

"Turn your eyes from me; they overwhelm me" (6:5, NIV)

The King, the risen glorious Savior of this entire world, speaks intimately to her. "Be alert, O my soul, for the preposterous word He births within me."

Remember, His entire life flow is incredible!

Flesh loves little, and possibly loves Him not at all. The human heart lacks all capacity to love the living God. But time with Him transforms the heart. He is resurrection life, and internally we are changed into a lover of the King. He now says of her and to her, "Your eyes captivate me."

What's going on here? "Christ in you" is going on—a word of God in Colossians 1:27 that I was taught in my discipleship classes. Certainly a great word the Apostle Paul was speaking, but so difficult to apply to my own personal devotion to the Lord. I was too hot or cold—not in any way a stand out.

"Oh, heart of mine, allow this Lover of my soul to captivate me!" (See Ephesians 1:17–23; Acts 26:18; Psalm 118:19–29.)

"Your hair is like a flock of goats moving down the slopes of Gilead. Your teeth are like a flock of ewe, that have come up from the washing, all of them bear twins, not one of them is bereaved" (6:5–6)

> *The beauty she wears on her head reflects the high places.*
> *Her heart flies there in the power of Your divine anointing.*
> *That private time with You behind closed doors opens so*
> *many more doors, drawing us into your glory.*

She possesses within her person glorious revelation of the risen King.

> *She possesses Your fullness. In You she lacks nothing.*

It's all true!

> Christ in you, the hope of glory.
>
> —COLOSSIANS 1:27

(See Revelation 3:20–4:4; Isaiah 2:3.)

"Your cheeks are like halves of a pomegranate behind your veil" (6:7)

As she lost Him for a time, her heart became more intense. She deepened her commitment to Him. In each instance His beauty and holiness is released more fully within her. Her countenance is saturated in His holiness…behind her veil.

Pomegranate is the fruit befitting the priesthood. Those who enter in behind the veil in the holy of holies to minister to the living God, wear this insignia embroidered on their clothing. It signifies the anointing of Christ's blood. His blood allows the birthing of the heart of the bride within very common people.

We designate the journey of our hearts, and He fulfills it as our High Priest. We never have to act spiritual again. He creates the authentic heart of His bride within us. We truly become walking miracles of His presence in His world. We enter into the holy of holies by a new and living way in the Bridegroom love of our Savior and Lord.

> Let my prayer be counted as incense before Thee, and
> the lifting of my hands as an evening sacrifice.
>
> —Psalm 141:2

(See Hebrews 10.)

"There are sixty queens and eighty concubines, and maidens without number. My dove, my perfect one, is only one, the darling of her mother, flawless to her that bore her. The maidens saw her and called her happy; the queens and concubines also, and they praised her" (6:8–9)

She is not identified by a group, no matter how special that group may be. She stands out because she is separated, or set apart. King

Solomon is making a distinction here as to his own ladies. They too were set apart for his pleasure alone.

Everyone who is associated with her knows that the substance of who she is draws them far beyond any earthly norm. He created her future title as the stand out; most beautiful among women. His word said this of her as one still fresh from the dark tents in 1:8. She did not enter His presence in this condition, but as one who was desperate for new life. She was not pretty in any way. But she was hungry!

(See Romans 1:4–6; 8:28–30, 9:25.)

"Who is this that looks forth like the dawn, fair as the moon, bright as the sun, terrible as an army with banners?" (6:10)

> *On a stage within our history, You, Father God, dramatically fought back as Your Son hung on that historical cross. His life flowed out of Him onto the earth upon which our lives are lived out. You took center stage and You won over man's singular problem of sin. You made the most dramatic statement ever made for the human heart.*
>
> *You won on that great day, but as yet still remain basically unknown or little known to the heart. You were altogether present at this world's dawn, but the inner darkness of the heart maintains its estrangement from You. And yet in this mass of humanity, You do find the hearts to call bride. And in so many ways they will look like you.*

Christ's presence is the actual presence of heaven's mighty army. With Christ living within us, we are not simply weak humans wandering this earth within the confines of fragile faith as well as ignorance. His presence is not only as the Lover of our hearts and souls but one who magnificently fights for the right to be glorified within our hearts.

> Some boast of chariots, and some of horses; but we boast of the name of the Lord our God.

—Psalm 20:7

Her faith is not simply a sweet feeling now and then. His presence is a mighty army! Satan attacks Him, and he meets the roar of the Lion!

> Day to day pours forth speech, and night to night declares knowledge. There is no speech nor are there words; their voice is not heard; yet their voice goes out through all the earth, and their words to the end of the world.
>
> —Psalm 19:2–4

(See John 8:56; Philippians 1:6; Psalms 90:12, 50:1–2, 15, 20:5–9.)

"I went down to the nut orchard to look at the blossoms of the valley, to see whether the vines had budded, whether the pomegranates were in blossom" (6:11)

In John 15:1 Jesus defines His Father as the husbandman of His vineyard. It's about glory production which He birthed within her. She now naturally assumes His caring role. It is her inner joy!

Are the pomegranates in bloom? Their blood red stain produces holiness. The fruit of the vine produces worship. Both bind us or weave all that we are into His beauty and glory. We are not being presumptuous. We are being called by His powerful voice filled with His Father's life. Perhaps the bride's strongest personal feature is her ability to love the living God, thereby fulfilling the first commandment. On which all the other commandments rest.

> …and you shall love the Lord your God with all your heart, and with all your soul, and with all your might. And these words which I command you this day shall be upon your heart.
>
> —Deuteronomy 6:5–6

(See John 15:1–11; Isaiah 5:1–4.)

"Before I was aware, my fancy set me in a chariot beside my prince" (6:12)

She naturally keeps His company. She is established within both worlds: the world of this present day as well as the world full of His glory.

In the Hebrew it suggests she find herself among the chariots of Amminadib; translated as a people of like mind. Chariots imply that these people are now heavenly creatures. This could also be the world occupied by His angels who serve and adore Him.

She is never the struggling lone Christian any place nor any time. She is now rooted within the cloud of witnesses described in Hebrews.

> Therefore, since we are surrounded by so great a cloud of witnesses, let us also lay aside every weight and sin which clings so closely, and let us run with perseverance the race that is set before us, looking to Jesus the pioneer and the one who perfects our faith.
>
> —Hebrews 12:1–2

In the fields of her natural roots, she struggled in an unproductive bitter fruit. But this no longer defines who she is. She lives and moves in utter rest in Him.

His Word is my resting place—the fruit of a hearing heart.

(See Psalms 110:3, 116:7–9, 55:6, Isaiah 11:10, 28:11–15, 55:12–13; Matthew 11:25–30.)

"Return, return, O Shulammite, return, return, that we may look upon you" (6:13)

Perhaps now in sheer panic the daughters of Jerusalem cry out! This may be their hour to make a commitment to the Son of a deeply personal loving God. She began all of this by crying for His kiss. Is this what they are willing to do? Or is this quality of intimacy still offensive in their relationship with the living God? Or is this dynamic revelation to the heart simply intriguing, and nothing more?

We throw open our souls to all sorts of casual intimacies in life, which end up owning us. Yet this one causes us pause. The distance between us and the living God stands. Am I saved? Yes, the blood of His cross reaches me! He reached out to me as one lost and separated. Then in The Song He romances my heart to draw as close to Him as possible. Kissing close!

"Heart of mine, stop the offense at His words: 'kisses of the mouth.'"

> *Father God, I do not and will not take offense at You, O Lover of my soul. I desire what she has, and all that she has experienced.*

(See Revelation 3:20–4:1.)

"Why should you look upon the Shulammite, as upon a dance between two armies?" (6:13)

Do they at all perceive not only her enormous beauty but her monstrous power as well? Again we are drawn to this revelation of His bride as His army. She alone may not be the army, but collectively she is created as one.

Who does she dance with but the heavenly host, the Lord of Hosts, and the great armies of heaven? Her relationship in Him is now described as a dance. No, as *the* dance!

> He made my feet like hind's feet, and set me secure on
> the heights. He trains my hands for war, so that my arms
> can bend a bow of bronze. Thou hast given me the shield
> of thy salvation and thy right hand supported me, and
> thy help made me great. Thou didst give a wide place for
> my steps under me, and my feet did not slip.
> —Psalm 18:33–36

This dance is rooted in dynamic worship. Her relationship in Him is now defined by her quality of worship. This may now be the dynamic as well as the definition of who she now is in Christ: one who worships body, soul, and spirit in His magnificent presence.

> Let them praise his name with dancing, making melody
> to him with timbrel and lyre. For the Lord takes plea-
> sure in His people; he adorns the humble with victory.
> Let the faithful exult in glory; let them sing for joy on
> their couches. Let the high praises of God be in their
> throats and two-edged swords in their hands.
>
> —Psalm 149:4–6

(See Psalms 149, 150:4; 2 Samuel 6:12–14; Exodus 15:20–21.)

"How graceful are your feet in sandals, O queenly maiden. Your rounded thighs are like jewels, the work of a master hand" (7:1)

> My steps have held fast to thy paths, my feet have not
> slipped.
>
> —Psalm 17:5

He has an admiring heart beholding the dance of His people, perhaps even *with* His people. In this dance she is transformed into His glorious beauty. But she is wearing sandals, just as He once did. In heaven and earth is where He dwells.

> After me comes he who is mightier than I, the thong
> of whose sandals I am not worthy to stoop down and
> untie.
>
> —Mark 1:8

When I direct my heart in song, then raising my hands now moving my feet before Him, He is delighted in my sacrifice of praise. But I don't have to do this. It doesn't save me. But it does strengthen my heart's commitment to Him. It does move me into the dynamic flow of His presence, which is glorious revelation.

I have been trying to learn to walk in Him for nearly fifty years, and I have been utterly ignorant of this relationship with His bride which He has desired to birth within me. I understood it theologically but never personally.

In a time of personal prayer in the sanctuary of a church, He spoke clearly to me. He said, "Please dance for Me." At first I was wholly embarrassed at the thought, then eventually obedient.

I was greatly blessed in an outpouring of revelation of how much He loved me. Most of my life I lived in ignorance of His passion. I began to discover intimate Bridegroom loving. Now I know that I am His bride—not at all based on the fact that I pursued Him with all of my heart. No, exactly the opposite is true! He aggressively pursued me!

This magnificent revelation is to take hold of us. And revelation in Him is never simply a principle of faith, but the dynamic of a glorious breathing person.

When He calls for me, what does He say? He says, "My love."

He says to me, "I have led you, and you have followed. I have sent you, and you have gone. You now dance with me, most beautiful among women."

> Singers and dancers alike say, "all my springs are in you."
> —Psalm 87

I am quite sure I am His favorite! I believe so! In the same way you, too, are His favorite, which is personal intimate knowledge which He births within each of us.

(See Jeremiah 31:10–14; Psalm 150:4; 2 Samuel 6:14; Matthew 11:16–20.)

"Your rounded thighs are like jewels, the work of a master hand" (7:1)

> For we are his workmanship, created in Christ Jesus for good works, which God prepared beforehand that we should walk in them.
> —Ephesians 2:10

Her intimacy in Him has poured glorious steel into her. She now stands in His glory. His inner strength birthed in all that she is, now appears more like jewels, or more like the radiance which is found in Him.

> Be watchful, stand firm in your faith, be courageous, be
> strong, let all that you do be done in love.
>
>   —1 Corinthians 16:13–14

> Thy right hand is filled with victory.
>
>   —Psalm 48:10

(See Romans 5:2; Galatians 5:1; Ephesians 6:11–14; Philippians 6:1; Psalm 48.)

"The work of a master hand" (7:1)

Now the master hand speaks freely and openly about her. Then The Song is essentially about a woman's heart? No, it's about the human heart. She is a figure of the bride found within His body, the church. We are created in God's image and His image is both male and female. His image incorporates all of humanity.

We are created for bridal union unto His Son, the glorious Bridegroom of history. My physical body clothes an interior body which participates fully in this heavenly union. I am created in a way which will naturally display His glory, as well as function on my planet in sandals similar to His. My heart will become operational.

All that I am was created to know Him intimately! All that I am is created to take supernatural steps in Him in living faith! Here I stand, whether in my ordinary circumstances here on earth or in the high places of His glory. I do know within my heart that He has birthed the power to stand when my faith is assaulted.

(See Isaiah 4:2–6, 61:3; Psalm 149:1–7.)

"Your navel is a rounded bowl that never lacks mixed wine. Your belly is a heap of wheat encircled with lilies" (7:2)

It's great knowledge, supernatural to the human heart. When He anoints us He does so body, soul, and spirit. All that we are receives the wine of heaven: His beautiful fullness! He is not offended at any part of our bodies, as we are. After all, He wore the same body parts.

Within the structure of His humanity, He comfortably served His Father fully—body, soul, and spirit.

In God's plan we are carefully created to house His glory. She is His storehouse of radiant life within His world. In the Hebrew *my soul* is translated as "my glory." This sheds some light as His glory is woven into every dimension of our beings. She is a storehouse of divine nourishment, which creates faith and knowledge, an anointed word or teaching, or simply a presence.

Wine and wheat speak of the Lord's Supper. God never designed this as an archaic tradition. No, His heart appoints this feast of life to birth new revelation within us. I possess deep within me the presence of His glorious life. I am a new creation! Revelation is never simply words, but more the entire substance of life!

> Therefore, if anyone is in Christ, he is a new creation; the old has passed away, behold the new has come.
>
> —2 CORINTHIANS 5:17

> I keep the Lord always before me; because he is at my right hand, I shall not be moved. Therefore my heart is glad, and my soul rejoices; my body dwells secure.
>
> —PSALM 16: 8–9

(See Galatians 3:6–9; John 6:25–35, 45–51; Psalm 104:14–15, 81:16.)

"Your two breasts are like two fawns, twins of a gazelle" (7:3)

The metaphor of twins of a gazelle speaks of those who know how to find life substance in the high places. The apostle John in the Book of Revelation teaches us about the Savior of this world, who is also the King of heaven. He knocks personally on the door of our hearts (3:20). This Lord and Savior, Bridegroom of the human heart, so much desires to spend intimate time within us. But He needs a quiet heart; even if the focus is weak, it will suffice.

His word is not always embedded in the form of a language. But is, I suspect, more associated with His presence. The message is freed from rhetoric, which is so limiting. The substance of this One who is breathing close defines the meaning of who I am. Our spending personal time with Him here on earth too often appears benign, bland, or of no benefit. Omnipresence does not define this special time. But two hearts moving together in Christ is His Bridegroom presence within the soul.

"O heart of mine, sit up and listen."

Open the eyes of our hearts and transform all our interior understandings as to who we truly are in you.

> We who first hoped in Christ have been destined to live for the praise of his glory.
>
> —Ephesians 1:12

(See Revelation 3:20–4:1; Ephesians 1:3–23, 17–23.)

"Your two breasts" (7:3)

Her two breasts are not only full but they also define her amazing beauty. She is full because He is full! There are two breasts which represent not only the fullness of Christ's own beauty, but also God's divine pairs.

> And the word became flesh and dwelt among us, full of grace and truth.
>
> —John 1:14

> Who redeems your life from the pit, who crowns you with steadfast love and mercy.
>
> —Psalm 103:4

> The Lord is merciful and gracious, slow to anger, and abounding in steadfast love.
>
> —Psalm 103:8

> Righteousness and justice are the foundation of thy throne; steadfast love and faithfulness go before thee.
>
> —Psalm 89:14; 103:8

> To the saints and faithful brethren in Christ at Colossae; grace to you and peace from God our Father.
>
> —COLOSSIANS 1:2; PHILIPPIANS 1:2

> So you, by the help of your God, return, hold fast to love and justice, faith and love, and for a helmet the hope of salvation.
>
> —1 THESSALONIANS 5:8

> Hold fast to love and justice, and wait continually for your God.
>
> —HOSEA 12:6

> But, since we belong to the day, let us be sober, and put on the breastplate of faith and love, and for a helmet the hope of salvation.
>
> —1 THESSALONIANS 5:9

His bride is fully equipped to serve her God in balanced wisdom. This balance reiterates that we serve a glorious God, not simply a list of platitudes. The bride's two breasts are intimately connected into His fullness.

> For in him the whole fullness of deity dwells bodily, and you have come to fullness of life in him, who is the head of all rule and authority.
>
> —COLOSSIANS 2:9–10

(See Ephesians 1:5; John 1:14; Acts 9:17; 2 Corinthians 1:20; Psalm 16:11, 36:7–8.)

"Your neck is like an ivory tower. Your eyes are pools of Heshbon, by the gates of Bath-rabbim" (7:4)

The neck, spiritually, represents persistence in the heart. She focused on Him in asking for His kisses. Later she ran after Him. But we never sensed running energy being expanded within her. She determined to run towards Him and then His Holy Spirit picked her up and carried her into intimacy in Him. She's running, yes, but He's transporting. I love this!

(See 1 Corinthians 9:26; Philippians 2:16; Hebrews 12:1; Psalm 133; Galatians 5:7.)

"Your eyes are pools in Heshbon" (7:4)

Pools are not flowing water unless the flow of water is deep below the surface. These pools were possibly large, deep reservoirs, tranquil and highly reflective.

In Song One she was telling Him that she grew up in trouble. Her vineyards were unproductive. She was stirred up within her soul as to who she was at that time, no doubt troubled water. She cried out, "Kiss me, draw me, and tell me! Help me and change me and love me and hear me and love me and kiss me!"

The result of these outcries and the time she has spent with Him have created pools within her being. Those who would draw near to the Bridegroom will find Him naturally reflected within her.

God chose this heart to launch the love song of the centuries. She's now a totally different person. The echo chambers of her heart quietly enjoy Him. Those around her perceive this deep reflection of joy which flows from Him. She fully understands this and quietly loves His presence. His joy sustains her as His Father's joy sustained His Son.

> …who, for the joy that was set before him endured the cross, despising the shame, and is seated at the right hand of the throne of God.
>
> —Hebrews 12:2

> A pool is open to the light of heaven, suggesting that this loved maiden had a heart before God which was notable for openness and purity. Her heart was not only free from the stirrings of any cloudy content but it was entirely at peace and perfectly reflected the will of God. "Heshbon," means "clever" or "understanding", and "Bath-rabbim" is defined as "a daughter of a large company." Thus the spouse of Christ has a spirit much in advance of the average believer.[1]
>
> —Watchman Nee

(See 1 Chronicles 15:16; Psalms 4:6–7, 5:11, 21:6; Luke 2:8–13.)

"Your head crowns you like Carmel, and your flowing locks are like purple: a king is held captive in the tresses" (7:5)

The fullness of glory is on her head. Her heart knows how to praise as she moves into worshiping Him. High praise covers her head! She wears His presence as a crown, which is the anointing of the Holy Spirit. The wonderful truth is the King adores her!

Praise and worship in our meetings were never designed simply to make us feel good, and yet they do. When we authentically worship our inner lives change, because our hearts are changed. A door is then thrown open to wear His glory! How and why? I don't know, but He throws open the door unto lavished love flowing over her. Wow! That should change me!

> *You need servant hearts within us. Nourish our hearts in Your presence. Change us body, soul, and spirit. Pour out Your resources over and through us.*

Yet these resources are nothing like those we know here on earth. They are totally different in that they are an overflow of heavenly life—the life of a precious Savior poured out for us, and then His Holy Spirit poured over and through us.

> *It never stops does it? You have so much to reveal in us. And it's not so much doing things as it is knowing Your presence, which wins our hearts. It's about You, the great Lover of our universe. But then you make it also about me, desperate for Your fullness!*

> Thou has said, 'seek ye my face.' My heart says to thee, 'thy face do I seek." Hide not thy face from me.
>
> —Psalm 27:8

(See Psalms 126, 67:1, 80:3.)

"How fair and pleasant you are, O loved one, delectable maiden" (7:6)

Living to know Him and to please Him reaps enormous rewards! Who else would ever love us to this depth, and who is able to?

Crying out to Him led her into His presence! She determined to search Him out, in this drawing her to Himself. His main purpose is to make her His servant? No, but to draw her into intimacy and to fully share His glory! He wants the heart of the bride birthed within each of us.

Does she develop a servant's heart, as important as this is? Absolutely! She serves Him with a heart filled with the overflowing revelation of His personal love. She knows Him deeply and reveals Him fully. Her focus is not so much in serving Him as it is in belonging to Him as His bride.

(See Jeremiah 29:11.)

"You are stately as a palm tree, and your breasts are like its clusters" (7:7)

> Grace has made her like the palm tree, the emblem of uprightness and fruitfulness. The fruit of the date-palm is more valued than bread by the oriental traveler, so great is its sustaining power. The fruit-bearing powers of the tree do not pass away; as age increases the fruit becomes more perfect as well as more abundant.[2]
>
> —Hudson Taylor

"I will climb the palm tree and lay hold of its branches. Oh, may your breasts be like clusters of the vine, and the scent of your breath like apples" (7:8)

To Israel, who was spoken of as God's bride, the palm branches were tokens of victory and peace. Israel waved them over our Savior as He made His grand entrance into Jerusalem. In this gesture they now confirmed His heavenly royalty. But their great King was first to become their Savior. These branches communicated to Israel that something great was about to take place. These branches were about appropriate praise. The joy of heaven, the fullness of salvation was about to flow into God's people. His complete joy was visiting them in the coming of a new day. God's lamb is about to save God's people.

He will not simply save His people but lead them into bridal love. Their lives would produce the sweet fruit of this union. Their personal lives would bear His glory to please Him and serve His world. He now finds within her, as well as within His people, heaven's fruit. But this fruit is from a tree which produces it in the most unlikely places.

How can weak unproductive lives produce His marvelous overflowing life?

She's involved in that journey of His lavished love and presence in every form it takes. She moved towards him in barrenness. What in the world did she have to offer Him? Her heart: and it has thrilled Him!

> The righteous flourish like the palm tree, and grow like a cedar in Lebanon. They are planted in the house of the Lord, they flourish in the courts of our God. They still bring forth fruit in old age, they are ever full of sap and green, to show that the Lord is upright; he is my rock, and there is no unrighteousness in him.
>
> —Psalm 92:12–14

(See John 15:5.)

"And your kisses like the best wine that goes down smoothly, gliding over lips and teeth" (7:9)

Lord, You thrill me and yet embarrass me. How could you ever say this to me in my present state? And still in The Song let us learn this about Him? He is not the least bit religious. He will whisper to us that which delights His heart. He is the most outrageous lover we will ever know!

The Song is essentially the journey into Your loving presence. Perfect intimacy into Your dynamic flow of life aimed within me. You have made every effort and accomplished every feat to win my heart. You are perfect intimacy merged into all that I am: perfect strength, sweet knowledge, and beauty; all that I would desire within my life time.

It is Your tenacious love for me which creates Your beauty, Your strength and productivity within me.

Kiss me with the kisses of your mouth, for Your love is sweeter than wine.

Your personal love is truly my life flow.

(See 1 Chronicles 22:9; Nehemiah 8:9–12; Psalm 84:2, 85:10, 107:30; Ecclesiastes 9:17; Isaiah 33:20; 1 Peter 3:4.)

"And your kisses" (7:9)

These kisses represent very selective intimacy within the framework of God's covenant love. Her kisses are for Him alone. Her kisses are the substance of His kisses. Therefore, now the strength of her love originates in His.

She is a focused heart. How He adores these hearts. She is not expanding any energy at all. But she is His!

> My mouth is filled with thy praise, and with thy glory
> all the day.
>
> —PSALM 71:8

He transforms her body, soul, and spirit. Every cell in this temple which defines who she is will know His presence and will glorify Him. What did all this create? Well for one thing, one excited Bridegroom!

(See Ephesians 1:15–23; Psalms 71:14–19, 145:16.)

"I am my beloved's and his desire is for me" (7:10)

The consummate confession of faith!

Engrave this within our hearts and souls.

How simply she says this. How much she is affirming His faithfulness. This is the ultimate confession of the human heart living in Christ. Could it be said in other ways? Of course!

We learn to love by being loved body, soul, and spirit. Who best to be loved by, than the Savior of our soul? We are too easily satisfied with casual love and with casual faith.

> *Open the eyes of our hearts to discern You in our days here on earth. I pray not to live recklessly ignorant of your personal presence.*
>
> *Such enormous beauty of heart and soul embraces each of us. Our hearts are changed in Your life flow. O personal Lover, how beautiful You are!*

Watchman Nee expresses this word of God in this way:

> She realizes that she now lives only for His pleasure and to be desired by Him and not to impose herself on Him. To live so as to be desirable to the Lord is the highest purpose of a believer's life.[3]

(See Song of Songs 1:4; Psalms 45:11, 85:10, 147:11, 73:22–28; Jeremiah 17:14.)

"Come, my beloved" (7:11)

We know the Lord loves us doctrinally, but seldom understand this experientially. As a church-going Christian do I ever serve Him in the context of this comment? As a Christian sitting in church Sunday by Sunday, I would have to confess I have only once experienced His passion personally in my heart.

His presence, His personal love dwelling within me touches and changes every memory which molds me. She has said nothing of the dark tents. They are no longer an issue. I want to become like her.

"Come, my beloved, let's spend this day together." The Song reveals to us that He's unable to resist this.

> The Lord, your God, is in your midst, a warrior who gives victory; he will rejoice over you with gladness, he

will renew you in his love; he will exult over you with loud singing as on a day of festival.

—Zephaniah 3:17

All the joy of heaven is rejoicing over you! Yes, *you*! (See Exodus 33:14.)

"Let us go forth into the fields" (7:11)

How should we define God's presence? In our world it's defined as omnipresent. Is this definition adequate? Or is it too generic?

But The Song is defining His presence in a far different light. It is not a presence directed towards an indifferent world. No, it's now concentrated on a particular people.

Now let's consider the quality of revelation flowing from this union as detailed in Song Three and Four. First, our interior union needs to allow this personal revelation to embrace us in much stronger attachments than those of our world.

We are submerged into His marvelous flow of life. I see it as a river in which I am invited to float on, not drown in. A presence surrounding me desiring to make Himself fully known. Not a presence designed to quench my unique qualities but to activate them. I now move in a deeply personal revelation of His presence and more in His personal love.

God says this about Jacob, who represents the common man facing all the problems and trials we face.

> They shall come and sing aloud in the height of Zion,
> and they shall be radiant over the goodness of the Lord,
> over the grain, the wine and the oil, and over the young
> flock and the herd; their life shall be a watered garden,
> and they shall languish no more.
>
> —Jeremiah 31:12

(See John 17:5; Acts 2:28, 3:19; Psalms 21:6, 95:2, 100:2 105:4, 139:7.)

"Come, my beloved, let us go forth into the fields" (7:11)

Why is she saying this and directing Him to do this? God didn't give her field orders. No, He gave her His heart! He loves these fields, and now so does she. She cannot stay out of them!

Strange isn't it? Her first encounter with Him was her outcry from the dark fields of life. She was lost and miserable. She was simply crying for someone to love her intimately: "Give me Your kisses!" She was focused on the Lord and His enormous ability to love the wounded. He was thrilled that this field worker was crying out for Him.

Now time spent in the loving presence of the Lord presents us with one so beautiful. Could her story also happen within us? She naturally radiates His presence.

Take notice of everything which has been birthed within her. Notice who she now is; and the wonderful truth is that she is not the least bit religious. She is genuinely being herself. However, it is a redeemed self in the beautiful Bridegroom presence of Christ.

All of this only took place because she was such a prize? Utter nonsense! She was lost and filthy in those fields of life. In Christ's Bridegroom presence we are radically loved and changed, and then presented to the Father as His.

Hers was never a trip, but a journey carefully overseen by God's loving presence. A trip simply means she goes some place and then returns to the same old place. No, the Father always yearned for her presence fully in His family. And she is now there as the bride of His Son.

"Come, my beloved, let us go forth into the fields and lodge in the villages" (7:11)

We need to learn to move in you, as natural as breathing.

She is doing this now. "Let us now go into your world." She says this to Him with such ease. This is not the result of a great personal faith. No, it's the natural outflow of union.

There was dimness of soul when she said to Him, "Turn my beloved" (2:17), go on and do what you need to do. Now she says, "Let *us*." She naturally displays this union.

> *I want my prayers now to begin with, "Let us." Be glorified in me, body, soul, and spirit.*

(See 1 Thessalonians 5:23–24; Colossians 3:1–4, 10, 16.)

"Let us go out early to the vineyards, and see whether the vines have budded" (7:12)

> *I love what You do. I love Your gardens. I love how they bloom and the fullness of their production. I love how You produce this within each of us.*

In The Song the human heart is described over and over again as His productive gardens. If the heart is not His, then we experience inner wastelands and our sin clings to us like mud.

She has said this so naturally, as if it were an everyday thing. The full dynamic of this union has become just this: an everyday thing!

> It is the spirit that gives life, the flesh is of no avail; the words that I have spoken to you are spirit and life.
>
> —John 6:63

(See Matthew 7:24–27; Luke 4:22, 21:33.)

"And the pomegranates are in bloom. There I will give you my love" (7:12)

The bride is a person set apart for one calling: to exalt the living God. Her Bridegroom Lover has completely fulfilled this, and thus He now seeks to fulfill this awesome role within us as well.

We speak of salvation as new birth, or continually being born anew in an ongoing work taking place within us. But never in terms of losing basic salvation over and over again. The ongoing work is moving into His full overflow of life—His glory.

Then He said, Lo, I have come to do thy will, O God,'
as it is written of me in the roll of the book.

—HEBREWS 10:7

He is the sovereign Lover, Savior, reigning King of our hearts and souls! Faith and revelation is substantially birthed within her heart and soul, as it is in us. Where she had been occupied by her own brokenness, she now serves Him with authority.

Pomegranates speak to our being inducted into His priesthood. This fruit is embroidered into their robes. She wears His glory now naturally birthed within her, as though embroidered. It is defining "Christ in you, the hope of glory" (Col. 1:27). Paul understood this.

She now possesses gold and diamonds within her spirit. Her confession of faith is exhibited in: "There I will give you my love. I will glorify you."

(See 1 Timothy 1:12–17; 1 Peter 1:13, 2:9–10; Psalm 72:18–19.)

"The mandrakes give forth fragrance, and over our doors are choice fruits, new as well as old, which I have laid up for you, O my beloved" (7:13)

The fragrance of His presence in His family and in His world is enormously powerful to reveal all that He is in the human heart. Fragrance is spoken of all the way through The Song. Fragrance is His presence and His beautiful presence is often defined as His powerful fragrance.

Simply seeing the ark of the covenant in the holy of holies and understanding the importance of its presence in our lives should alone change us. But there is added the fragrance of His presence and His eternal love for us. We are never destined to simply know something about Him. We are drawn to Him, in every way, to experience this intimacy.[1]

The fragrance of a dead or dying body is awful! We immediately run from it! But His fullness of life in overflowing fragrance is just the opposite. We run towards Him!

This book awakens this truth within us. His truth is never simply a principle or a moral ethic; but even more, a divine beating heart, a tsunami of His powerful love, uprooting the blights which take liberties in defining who we are.

I also see this in the presence of the fullness of the Holy Spirit working in us in so many unknown ways. He is God's dynamic presence in surrounding us, drawing us in until our hearts perceive His pleasure. Until His love fully wins within us His Lord's bride. (See 1 Corinthians 3:14–15, 13:13; 2 Timothy 2:13.)

"O that you were like a brother to me, that nursed at my mother's breast. If I met you outside, I would kiss you, and none would despise me" (8:1)

> *How many ways may I relate to You? How many ways may I be found in You? How many ways may I learn to worship You?*
>
> *It is good that our humanity appreciates your humanity. After all, You burst into our history as a baby, found in a stable for donkeys. Well, in our natural state we may be just that: the donkeys.*
>
> *You then grew as a Son, even then about His Father's business. At a young age You were even involved in heaven's call on Your heart. Your hands built furniture, as well as eagerly healed the human soul. We possess a meager vision of Your divinity.*
>
> *In our skin You merged heaven into earth. You truly are a perfect Lover and Savior of all that we are, inwardly as well as outwardly. There is no one better or more capable than You!*

The Song lets revelation flow. The Song lifts our hearts and souls into the treasure house of our Savior and Lord, Jesus Christ. (See Philippians 4:4–7; Ephesians 6:10–20.)

"I would lead you and bring you into the house of my mother, and into the chamber of her that conceived me" (8:2)

I am born of God and filled with His enormous life-giving Spirit. That is who I am! She is declaring her roots as one birthed in supernatural strength and love: His, from her inception and possibly before that.

> Nevertheless I am continually with thee; thou dost hold my right hand. Thou dost guide me with thy counsel, and afterward thou wilt receive me to glory. Whom have I in heaven but thee? And there is nothing upon earth that I desire besides thee. My flesh and my heart may fail, but God is the strength of my heart and my portion for ever.
>
> —PSALM 73: 23–26

A personal confession she has allowed to be sowed deeply within her heart and soul.

(See Ephesians 3:14–21.)

"And into the chamber of her that conceived me" (8:2)

The soul can get lost so easily. The heart is the anchor!

> *I would satisfy Your heart in me. I was created to love You, know You as fully as possible. And build a relationship with You that would ultimately draw me far beyond myself. In this relationship You would call me "My love." You would honor me in Your Father's great presence as your bride.*
>
> *Oh, Father, You have destined us for such greatness in You. We are not only destined for Your heaven but also as one carefully chosen to know You and serve You as one living in intimacy; as well as with One who adores us, Your Son.*

*No one in my earth's journey was able to pull this off
with fortitude. No one! The meaning of my journey in life
is found in You alone!*

(See 1 Corinthians 1:4–9.)

"I would give you spiced wine to drink, the juice of my pomegranates" (8:2)

*Holiness is Your fruit birthed within me, and I now serve
You from this vine—the pomegranate substance of my life,
planted within me from the beginning to bear Your image.
From the beginning I was chosen by You and Your Father
to bear Your glory. From the very beginning Your personal
calling in me was created to later be established.*

*I was never to be an irrelevant incident in history. This
meaning never defined who I am; from the very beginning
I was destined to be the bride of glory.*

> To them God chose to make known how great among
> the gentiles are the riches of the glory of this mystery,
> which is Christ in you, the hope of glory.
>
> —COLOSSIANS 1:27

"O that his left hand were under my head, and that his right hand embraced me" (8:3)

This is one definition of Christ's love and salvation poured into
us and poured over us. In the embrace of God's left hand, I stand
perfect before Him. That, in itself, is an enormous miracle! This, in
itself, creates rest in my heart and soul. My life is not an odyssey,
entangled in a futile struggle of proving how good I am. He did not
appoint me to travel that route.

Her journey in Christ is appointed to teach us about ours. It's all
about His fullness of life and glory, His glory manifested within us.
We are that important to Him!

> *I ask you for many things, but your desire is to loose within me an enormous flow of life and glory which will make You known. Amen.*

(See Psalms 22:22–31, 86:8–13; Ephesians 1:18; Romans 8:19–21.)

"I adjure you, O daughters of Jerusalem, that you stir not up nor awaken love until it pleases" (8:4)

Every season appointed unto her life requires a season of rest. A good wine must sit for a season. So much revelation has flowed into her. Her relationship in Him has expanded fully into the heavenly places. She must sit and rest, to absorb all that which has been birthed within her. His new life, His glory and love for the Father, His saving us so as to birth His bride within us, and this list goes on for eternity.

> I will give thanks to the Lord with my whole heart; I will tell of all thy wonderful deeds. I will be glad and exult in thee, I will sing praise to thy name, O Most High.
>
> —Psalm 9:1

An old saint, Bernard of Clairveaux, says it this way:

> Only the touch of the Spirit can inspire a song like this, and only personal experience can unfold its meaning. Let those who are versed in the mystery revel in it; let all others burn with desire rather to attain to this experience than merely to learn about it. For it is not a melody that resounds abroad but the very music of the heart, not a trilling on the lips but an inward pulsing of delight, a harmony not of voices but of wills. It is a tune you will not hear in the streets, these notes do not sound where crowds assemble; only the singer hears it and the one to whom he sings....the lover and the beloved.[4]

(See Psalms 139:17–18, 46:10; Exodus 14:14.)

Song Five

Glorious Union

8:5–8:14

*H*OW CAN WE ever know this song without experiencing His kisses, His caresses of the soul, His indomitable daily presence within our lives? Not as one seeking to control us, but rather seeking to love us as fully as we allow Him too. As one seeking to present Himself worthy to trust and to lean upon.

> So then, there remains a Sabbath rest for the people of God.
>
> —HEBREWS 4:8

> Beginning in Section One (1:2–2:7) with the unsatisfied longings of an espoused one, longings which could only be met by her unreserved surrender to the Bridegroom of her soul. We find that when the surrender was made, instead of the cross she had so much feared she found a King, the King of Love, who both satisfied her deepest longings, and found His own satisfaction in her.[1]
>
> —J. HUDSON TAYLOR

You are calling cold, distracted, wounded hearts on this journey of Your loving kisses. You choose us long before we ever choose You. The human condition always gets in the way. Because, Lord, what we want is not about You. It's all that other stuff we long for. It's all that other stuff that

155

we believe will give us happiness. But today I know I need grace and revelation lavished upon me.

The world sends me on a mission of pure toil. What do I get in Your presence? You draw me to Yourself and to Your Father's side. You lavish within me Your life forces. With us it's more about personal happiness. With You it's about my experiencing the fullness of Your presence.

The appointed Lover of my soul wore sandals as I do. His feet became dirty, just as mine do. The One who seeks my heart is very much like me; body, soul, and spirit. He also walks with wounded feet and a wounded heart. In so many ways He is just like us.

He was wounded for our transgressions. He carried my wounds to the cross. He took all my bruises with Him. Today our soldiers carry the wounds of our nation.

He restores my soul. He wins my heart and trust. He leads me beside still water. He is the Lover and Savior of my heart and soul.

I am educated. I have traveled the world over, but I am slow to discern Your kisses. And I am slowly learning to lean into Your arms.

This is my life journey appointed to immeasurable personal revelation centered within His life flow, which rises out from a heart who will not let me go; no matter how often I let Him go.

The God of the universe did not choose to give us a religious experience. He did not choose to simply give us a set of rules to live by. No, He's chosen to give us so much more! Man's relationship with this God is not based on our own personal worth, beauty, goodness, talents, commitment, or connections.

He has birthed a relationship within the center of our beings. It is not simply one of child to a father or servant to a master, but far more. This relationship defines an intimate alliance of heaven and earth—the closest possible between God and man. He loves revealing His Son to His world. And His world is not so much geographical places, but more the heart and soul of His people; or perhaps the heart and soul of one repugnant field worker.

> May God be gracious to us and bless us and make his
> face to shine upon us, that thy way may be known upon
> the earth, thy saving power among all nations.
>
> —PSALM 67:1–2

This woman of The Song has accomplished so much. The word now describes her as terrible as an army with banners. An army poised to fight, to win, to conquer, and to reveal the King of glory. An army poised to establish His kingdom reign.

He never charged her to posses the strength of an army. But He did, first of all, confront her to desire His kisses of the mouth. How do we reconcile kisses with armies? With some difficulty!

This song does not oblige nor accommodate the natural mind. We must be open to receive the illumination of the Holy Spirit. His reign and His world has little similarity to ours. And yet how much He desires we know Him in magnified authenticity. For this reason it is not focused on the female heart alone. But this journey of faith is destined for every heart.

On the mission field we experienced such darkness from an army of demons. But now we associate in His army of angel warriors. We will fight these battles and win.

But He's after the human heart. Not simply one time encounters, but profound intimacy. He's won when He calls us bride; when He calls us "My love" and we answer "my beloved." Then He's won, and He is glorified.

She first collapsed into His embrace in Song One; an established requirement. Now she leans, pressing into all that He is as the lover in her life. The heart who has never sought His intimacy and is thoroughly turned off at the thought of His kisses will not grasp His glory.

The heart who says, "Kiss me with the kisses of Your mouth," will move quickly into intimate revelation of heart and soul. This heart will increasingly know His glory. This heart will increasingly receive personal revelations of how active this Bridegroom is in his or her life; even if this heart doesn't begin to grasp the deeper message of His "kisses."

Whose heart hungers the most for this union? Who gave up the most? Who worked the hardest? This answer is found in the Father's Heart. He needed a glorious Bridegroom King which He found in His Son. Before that He needed a sacrificial Lamb, which he found in His Son's heart. His Son was ready, as fully man and fully God, to give everything required to establish this union of heaven and earth.

But the most amazing part of this divine equation is that it centers upon you and me. We are that important in God's glorious plan. Not our works, and possibly not our worship, as important as they are; but you and I, as those birthed in His image—those of us who have wandered in this wilderness of life. We wear the scars which wandering produces. We connect when she says, "I am dark like the tents of Kedar." And yet His glorious gaze finds us long before we discern Him.

When God hovered over you in your mother's womb, He carefully formed in you wonderful qualities that would glorify Him, the living God. You were no accident and you were never unwanted. These may have been labels placed on you at your birth. The two actors who allowed this creation defining "you" were possibly not at all pleased with your presence. But your family in heaven shouted for joy at your entrance into God's world.

You may now bear the scars as one from the dark tents. But God has created for you a way out. It is possible you are no different than the heart who cried out for more of God's personal love in Song One.

Why does He bother? Leave it be! No way! His planned future designated for each of us is too great and too glorious. He has appointed to each one of us a personal knowledge of His heart.

> Bless our God, O peoples, let the sound of his praise be
> heard, who has kept us among the living and has not let
> our feet slip.
>
> —Psalm 66:8–9

What do I honestly expect to transpire in my relationship in Christ? My own expectations hover near the poverty line. I have never anticipated much more than the fact that He saved me. And when I die I will spend eternity with Him. This alone is glorious! But there is still much more! He's opened the door to a fullness of life in Him now on earth.

The truth is my Bridegroom Lover has wrestled heaven and hell to birth within me this glorious new name. The Joy of heaven waits to call me His bride. Our personal faith is about married love, not casual encounters or one night stands. It's about our hearts moving into the fullness of God's heart swallowing up everything which ambushes this holy calling within us. Winning my heart may require His army. He says, "Not a problem!"

> His divine power has granted to us all things that
> pertain to life and godliness, through the knowledge of
> him who called us to his own glory and excellence.
>
> —1 Peter 3–4

"Who is that coming up from the wilderness, leaning upon her beloved?" (8:5)

Who is this, coming up from the wilderness? One who has learned to walk leaning on Him. This may be one of the most important revelations concerning the Bride. She knows how to lean, and I suspect she loves doing it.

Leaning absorbs His life flow. Leaning requires we discern His presence. By faith we receive His plan of salvation. We grow in the grace and the knowledge of the Bridegroom of the heart.

The sacrifice of praise becomes a reality in my prayer relationship to Him. And I then lean more. Leaning becomes a natural response in my faith life. I then experience His lifting me into Holy Spirit worship in Him. Here I absorb gold; authentic life flowing from God's presence through His Bridegroom son—to me, in me, for me. He's calls me bride.

> O Lord, who shall sojourn in thy tent? Who shall dwell
> on thy holy hill?
>
> —Psalm 15:1

In a heart clothed in darkness, she cried out. His loving Spirit transported her into Bridegroom presence. He lavished on her His full attention. Have we ever discerned this taking place within our own spiritual journeys or have we been too busy? I now realize I have never expected Him to focus personally on me. It never crossed my mind; therefore, I focused less on Him.

She pursued and followed Him, more in inner weakness than committed strength. She found Him, then lost Him, wandered about a bit, and then again found a renewed focus in Him. However, I suspect this relationship was sustained more in His commitment than in hers. He possessed the vision of making her His bride. I am not sure she clearly understood this.

Learning to lean on Him requires I spend more time in Him. Truly He is my shield, my wisdom, my strength in every dimension of life. He is my tower, my safe place. He provides within me the life of the Holy Spirit who perfectly glorifies His Father. He does all of this within the framework of who I am.

And Lord, it's such a fragile framework I am offering to you.

> Upon thee I have leaned from my birth; thou art he who
> took me from my mother's womb. My praise is continu-
> ally of thee.
>
> —Psalm 71:6

> The nations shall see your vindication, and all the kings
> your glory; and you shall be called by a new name which
> the mouth of the Lord will give. You shall be a crown of
> beauty in the hand of the Lord, and a royal diadem in
> the hand of your God.
>
> —Isaiah 62:2–3

Isaiah 10:20-23, 62:1-12, Proverbs 2:1-6, 3:5,6, Colossians 1:9-, Jeremiah 33:3.

"Under the apple tree I awakened you. There your mother was in travail with you, there she who bore you was in travail" (8:5)

"Under the apple tree, under the covering of my personal care for you, I was involved even at your birth. From your inception I have known you. I have been awakening your heart and soul towards me as you grew. You were always destined for this special relationship in me from the very beginning. I've always called you 'My love.'"

But He now says, "Married love in Me requires your commitment as well. Because of the enormous personal value of this relationship, I will not take you hostage. I will wait and love you as deeply and personally as I can, until you say, 'Yes'; until you say, 'More.'"

In God's perfect garden Adam and Eve were enticed to eat the fruit of the tree of the knowledge of good and evil. As a result we lost perfect fellowship with the living God. Our hearts were then embraced by sin and death.

His calling in our lives is directed toward our hearts. His calling requires intimacy. His calling involves heart kisses. He is the Lover of our soul. He fully redeems us.

> And this is eternal life, that they know thee the only
> true God, and Jesus Christ whom thou hast sent.
> —JOHN 17:3

I have understood this truth for years. But I have never grasped it as to my becoming Your bride. My wandering heart never grasped this intimacy birthed within me, which You so desire. You draw me so far beyond who I now am, and equally further from those old tents.

How well should I know you?

In the fullness of intimacy on His terms.

> Keep me as the apple of your eye; hide me in the shadow
> of your wings.
>
> —Psalm 17:8

(See Ephesians 4:17–24; Romans 8:1–11.)

"Under the apple tree he awakened me" (8:5)

The Holy Spirit births the bride within God's people. He performs the work of the Father's heart even from the beginning. He gazed at my destiny, and my heavenly Father became excited over me.

It's always about His work taking place within us—His being allowed to intimately perform His handiwork and to create His beauty, which glorifies His Son.

I never earned this special attention, but I am cherished. It's corny, isn't it? No, His love is never this. My own personal commitment to Christ might be described this way. If my love is mostly an emotional high and this is all I really want—an emotional experience and not this person—then perhaps it is trite.

You might label it as fatuous. But the current of His love, the embodiment of His life flow, is genuine. And we can build our lives, inside and out, on His commitment within us. Here I rest; here I lean. And His kisses release this journey in me, into His fullness.

> *Under the tree of life, You first became our Savior as God's Lamb. You entered our world as perfect man. You then became the exalted King of glory. Now you are the Bridegroom of our hearts. You called us, and made it authentic.*

> But I have trusted in thy steadfast love; my heart shall
> rejoice in thy salvation. I will sing to the Lord, because
> he has dealt bountifully with me.
>
> —Psalm 13:5

(See Romans 4:16–17, Psalms 116:7, 75:1; Revelation 22:16–17.)

"Set me as a seal upon your heart" (8:6)

Set me as a seal upon your heart. Perform this work of grace within me. Make this attachment solid so that I love what you love. Set me, all that I am, as a seal to your glory. Create in me an authentic oneness in you.

> One thing have I asked of the Lord, that will I seek after; that I may dwell in the house of the Lord all the days of my life, to behold the beauty of the Lord, and to inquire in his temple.
>
> —PSALM 27:4

I am an earth traveler and one who is prone to wander, as well as one with diverse attention spans.

Set me as a seal on Your heart. Create this confession of faith within me. I am not stable enough; but, Lord, You are.

> Behold, thou desirest truth in the inward being; therefore teach me wisdom in my secret heart.
>
> —PSALM 51:6

Set me firmly in the flow of Your love for the Father. May I authentically please Him in all that I do and am. Only You, Savior, Bridegroom of my heart and soul, are able to perform this within me. Why does Your love focus on such weak people who truly love to wander?

You created the wedding between us and Your Son. You chose us to enter into this union long before we ever chose You. Now we say yes! Absolutely yes to You to participate body, soul, and spirit into Christ's life flow.

> May the God of peace himself sanctify you wholly; and may your spirit and soul and body be kept sound and blameless at the coming of our Lord Jesus Christ. He who calls you is faithful, and he will do it.
>
> —1 THESSALONIANS 5:23–24

"Set me as a seal upon your heart" (8:6)

> *We've enjoyed Your glory in observing Your mountain ranges, ocean views, and glorious sunsets. We know You are beautiful! I might have prayed, "Please make me beautiful like a sunset." But this would never be answered. My heart is not asking for enough.*
>
> *Allow me to share in Your Son's glory as His bride.*

The angels of heaven now shout enormous praise in that she's finally gotten it. A voluminous yes roars through heaven for God's people have finally gotten it! No sunsets established within you.

Our lives are all about this relationship. And what is the relationship? Chosen bride for heaven's Bridegroom.

> ...and to know the love of Christ which surpasses knowledge, that you may be filled with all the fullness of God.
>
> —Ephesians 3:19

"Set me as a seal upon your heart" (8:6)

"Set me as a seal" is intense loving with an intense heart. Now she's serious. He's always been serious. He will love those made in His image. He will seek us out in a river of life, the blood of His Son.

The Bridegroom of the human heart continually knocks on the door of our heart to create interior and ongoing pleasure of His presence within us. (See Revelation 3:20.)

He's not a tease. He is intense concerning this relationship. He's in love with you and me. He's not there to simply give us orders or His message for the day or simply to say something to us. But within all that He is, He is the message. He is the fullness of life flowing into us. He is heart knowledge. His quality of knowledge is His interior kisses of the heart and soul. His presence within us is truly His kisses. His presence authenticates His personal love for each of us.

> Now the Lord is the Spirit, and where the Spirit of the
> Lord is, there is freedom. And we all, with unveiled face,
> beholding the glory of the Lord, are being changed into
> his likeness from one degree of glory to another; for this
> comes from the Lord who is the Spirit.
>
> —2 CORINTHIANS 3:17–18

> Thou art my hiding place and my shield; I hope in thy
> word.
>
> —PSALM 119:114

(See Psalms 119:103, 128–130, 133, 151, 166.)

"As a seal upon your arm; for love is as strong as death, jealousy is cruel as the grave. Its flashes are flashes of fire" (8:6)

This seal is the strongest connection possible. The sealant is the blood of Christ, the Bridegroom of the human heart. He completes all that I am. However, the seal is also interpreted as a signet ring; a ring binding two hearts together—a symbol of an inseparable connection, of two becoming one.

Her profound statement is "for love is as strong as death." Good news in that the death forces from the dark tents are fully released from every aspect of her being, and she is as free as she can be while still on earth. Moving into His chambers of the fullness of His love has transformed who she is in every way. Love conquers, His love wins! And in all this she leans.

> And in that day says the Lord, you will call me, 'my
> husband,' and no longer will you call me, 'my baal.'"
>
> —HOSEA 2:16–17

(See Psalms 9, 14–16; Hosea 2:16–23.)

"For love is strong as death, jealously is cruel as the grave. Its flashes are flashes of fire" (8:6)

She is not simply in a pleasant relationship, but far more. As His bride she has moved more fully into His glory and holiness. This is often manifested as fire. It is often seen as an anointing of fire which we experience as God's people. This marriage captures all of heaven's attention and resources.

Leaning absorbs His life flow. When I move beyond a sacrifice of praise, His Spirit lifts me into authentic worship, which draws me closer to His Father's throne. Be sure to keep pencil and paper handy for there will be a flow of thought directed into you. It is a revelation of His glory released in you. Here I absorb gold, His authentic life flow. These are His kisses of the mouth directed in me.

But God is out to win the human heart; and this means war! She has married the captain of God's armies, and she is now fully involved.

> They shall speak of the glory of thy kingdom, and tell of thy power, to make known to the sons of men thy mighty deeds, and the glorious splendor of thy kingdom.
>
> —Psalm 145:11–12

> His glory covered the heavens, and the earth was full of his praise.
>
> —Habakkuk 3:4

(See Psalms 13:5; 119:171–175, 145, 31:19; Hebrews 10.)

"Many waters cannot quench love, neither can floods drown it. If a man offered for love all the wealth of his house, it would be utterly scorned" **(8:7)**

Human love alone cannot make such an intense commitment to the living God. In all that we are, we need His enormous strength to draw us fully into this quality of devotion.

> *Through service, worship, or anything else that we might do which is spiritual, I cannot buy Your love. I can only receive it.*

The most we are able to do is to say yes over and over again to this lover's advancements.

> *Yes! And more yes's to You! Have Your way in me!*

A tsunami makes a final statement of death and destruction on everything in its path. No debate, it wins! Divine love is as strong as death! The battle rages on for the human heart!

The same is so true concerning God's river of life flowing out from His glorified Son. This river drowns sin and death, and it will restore this world to His Father.

> Oh send out thy light and thy truth; let them lead me, let them bring me to thy holy hill and to thy dwelling. Then I will go to the altar of God, to God my exceeding joy; and I will praise thee with the lyre, O God, my God.
>
> —Psalm 43:3–4

The bride now leans on the powerful Bridegroom Son. What she now expects in her natural flow of life is to be fully anointed in the supernatural love of the Father. His Son will be glorified whether on earth or in heaven. Jesus is Lord!

> …and designated Son of God in power according to the Spirit of holiness by his resurrection from the dead, Jesus Christ our Lord, through whom we have received grace and apostleship to bring about the obedience of faith for the sake of his name among all nations, including yourselves who are called to belong to Jesus Christ.
>
> —Romans 1:4–6

(See Romans 5:1–5, 8:37–39, 9:25–26; Ephesians 3:14–21.)

"If a man offered for love all the wealth of his house, it would be utterly scorned" (8:7)

She is exalted in her relationship with the Bridegroom Son. Up to now His greatest competition here on earth was human glory, which so easily captures our attention to the point that we live for it.

We don't buy this exalted relationship in Him. We don't earn it or deserve it. It was God's choice from the very beginning to choose us, than graciously wait until we choose Him.

Love is on center stage, not ours but His. His love is fully capable of winning our love.

> *You are more than enough. Your presence, Your favor with the Father is more than enough whether on earth or in heaven. Your presence alone lavishes on us all that we need in this present hour.*

What are those kisses we are to ask for, anyway? For one, I know they are sweet revelations of my alliance in Him. They are His whispers within my heart, birthing the personal knowledge of His glory within me.

(See Luke 2:20, 5:25, 18:42, 46; 1 Corinthians 2:7–13.)

"We have a little sister, and she has no breasts. What shall we do for our sister, on the day she is spoken for?" (8:8)

Even before bridal love and union it is possible, His deeper work is taking place. We may seem shallow, especially in the realm of our personal faith, but He who is rich works within us. Selah!

Longing to become His bride calls us far beyond and way outside of our normal flesh life. At some point, when we turn to focus on Him, He is able to draw us into His journey to become fully His. She did. The followers had not.

"Draw me after you and I will run" (1:4).

The lady from the dark tents said this. The daughters did not.

(See Psalms 101:6, 128:1; John 8:12; Romans 6:4.)

"If she is a wall, we will build upon her a battlement of silver; but if she is a door, we will enclose her with boards of cedar" (8:9)

As a wall she is a foundation not only for herself but for others as well. She is a life which will be built upon with solid heavenly life structures. He says He will build upon her towers of shining silver. This reflects His work within her to show forth His glory in the landscape of her life.

This building within us is always supernatural. It is essentially the work of the Holy Spirit. But He does need our cooperation.

Sweat and tears are not mentioned in this book. But so much has taken place within a common person's life. He is so capable and strong! He is sent out to do the tough work. Utterly amazing! The Holy Spirit is so good at what He does. He fully glorifies the hearts of the Father and His Son within us. Wow! Selah!

We will always be surrounded by those who as yet are not equipped to nurture. This young person has undeveloped breasts, a feature which allows us to build into the lives of others. But, nevertheless, the building within her goes on.

If she is an entrance then she will be constructed with cedar, a wood created from a tree of deep roots. This tree stands in the strongest storms and it is a wood which does not decay.

His work within her is always about Him. His work is not on and off again. His work establishes eternity in us and blesses our family tree. His work is divine revelation taking root.

Is this simply about a door and cedar planks? No, it's about His glory found in His people. Unfortunately, throughout our days we don't think about Him often because we don't know Him that well. This song was written to win our hearts fully to Him—as long as it takes.

Silver and cedar declare His eternal beauty and glory. Even now this young one is destined to become the bride. Even now she is on this journey; but perhaps, as yet, she doesn't know it.

(1 Kings 6:8–15; 2 Chronicles 2:1–6; Psalm 92:12–15.)

"I am a wall, and my breasts are like towers; thus I have become in his eyes like one bringing contentment" (8:10, NIV)

> *You are rock solid reality. You don't mess with our hearts to deceive us or to simply fill us with some good feelings.*

Your glorious presence first builds within us a solid foun-dation. We are not the cornerstone which establishes Your church in all the strength and power of heaven. But as His bride we are established very close to where He is.

> Lead thou me to the rock that is higher than I; for thou art my refuge, a strong tower against the enemy.
>
> —Psalm 61:2–3

The wall, or foundation, plus the towers of army strength maintains His peace. His peace, His union within her is the best contentment of mind and soul we could ever hope to experience in this world.

> Peace I leave with you; my peace I give to you; not as the world gives do I give to you. Let not your hearts be troubled, neither let them be afraid.
>
> —John 14:27

His peace is that state of tranquility, composure, and serenity often procured through victory in conflict and war. He has won for us and in us a powerful dynamic peace. It is not ludicrous! It is placing our feet on heaven's rock. Jesus spoke about being careful to build our lives upon the rock and not on sand. The rock represents His eternal strength and power designated to be a reality within us.

The rock represents His commitment to God's people. We can rest and trust His commitment when ours becomes soft.

(See Matthew 7:26; Psalm 85:10, 122:6–7; Isaiah 26:3.)

"I was a wall, and my breasts are like towers" (8:10)

These heavenly towers are the work of the Holy Spirit within us. They allow us to see far beyond ourselves. They are a point of visions. They reach into the heavenly places. Watchtowers lift us far beyond life's circumstances. We are not to be subject to the continued stress which life creates. There are special places we are to fellowship with the Holy Spirit away from the domination of the world we live in.

This place is very private, strong, and safe, and it has been estab-

lished within the heart. In quietness we read the scriptures, alert to
the interior voice of the Holy Spirit teaching us. I suspect He builds
the walls and the towers. The rock solid Word is His mortar, and
we may be the bricks whose interior substance has been radically
transformed.

I love the towers! I believe they can be built very high. They are
the place of visions.

> The name of the Lord is a strong tower; the righteous
> man runs into it and is safe.
>
> —PROVERBS 18:10

> I will take my stand to watch, and station myself on
> the tower, and look forth to see what he will say to me,
> and what I will answer concerning my complaint. And
> the Lord answered me; "Write the vision; make it plain
> upon tablets, so he may run who reads it.
>
> —HABAKKUK 2:1–2

> I call to thee, when my heart is faint. Lead thou me to
> the rock that is higher than I; for thou art my refuge, a
> strong tower against the enemy.
>
> —PSALM 61:1–3

(See 2 Kings 18:1–8; Isaiah 21:1–12.)

"Solomon had a vineyard at Baal Hamon; he let out the vineyard to keepers; each one was to bring for its fruit a thousand pieces of silver" (8:11)

The talents of Solomon are broad. God lavished upon him enormous wisdom in every area of life. Today he would hold degrees in
most academic disciplines. He would be held in the highest esteem
as he was in his world.

As a horticulturist his gardens were famous. He sees fruit as a
gift from God in the same way as we perceive Christ's productive
strength and beauty within us. It does belong to the Father.

Awaken the faith within us to first identify what You have produced, and then to fully love You and give You all the glory.

> If you abide in me, and my words abide in you, ask whatever you will, and it shall be done for you, By this my Father is glorified, that you bear much fruit, and so prove to be my disciples.
>
> —John 15:7–8

As the family of God we grow in faith due to the productive work others have accomplished within our vineyards. The first fruit glorifies the Lord. This is the interest paid for the talents freely given by Him. He receives the glory, and He allows us to share in it as one leaning on Him.

How do we now describe this person whose roots began in the dark tents of life? She is one who travels with heaven's armies, and I suspect at times gives the orders to launch the attack. She is also found exquisitely beautiful in Solomon's gardens. Plus, she teaches how important it is to learn to lean on the Lord of Glory in all the aspects of daily life.

> He who abides in me, and I in him, he it is that bears much fruit, for apart from me you can do nothing.
>
> —John 15:5

(See John 15:1; Psalms 91:1, 125:1; Haggai 2:4–9.)

"My vineyard, my very own, is for myself" (8:12)

There is a partnership established here. Not as one only receiving orders from the throne, but more as one adored by the Bridegroom King of heaven.

As a Christian seeking to grow in the knowledge of the living God, I had never perceived any of this in my journey of faith, except in The Song. I am adored, as you are! The Lord led me years ago into this odyssey of His personal love life destined for me.

I have never cared for poetry that much, so I was not drawn to

The Song. But when I began to dive into it, I discovered a passion released into me and for me, which I had never before experienced. The living God adores me!

How is it we find ourselves in the presence of the reigning God of the universe? First the journey leads us into intimacy with the Bridegroom. It begins in Revelation 3:20. This word challenges us to hear what the Holy Spirit is saying to us. He knocks personally on the door of the heart. He says, "Allow Me to abide there within you, in closed off solitude."

What will go on in there? What will be produced within us is clearly seen in Songs Three, Four, and Five. She absorbs His nature, and I suspect new birth is always taking place within her all the days of her life.

> Let us then with confidence draw near to the throne of grace, that we may receive mercy and find grace to help in a time of need.
>
> —HEBREWS 4:16

(See Hebrews 7:25, 10:22; Ephesians 1:17–23; Revelation 3:20–4:1.)

"You, O Solomon, may have the thousand, and the keepers of the fruit two hundred" (8:12)

Baal Hamon means "lord of the multitude." I am never to see myself as the lone Christian out to make my mark. No, I travel with a multitude, worldwide, in the knowledge of His grace.

We all are in the fruit-production business, and the result of our crops is to give the first tithe to glorify Him. It's about His life-giving love, but it also is about us as the soil for His beauty and glory within us.

(See Psalm 65:9–13; 1 Corinthians 3:6–7; Colossians 2:19.)

"O you who dwell in the gardens, my companions are listening for your voice; let me hear it" (8:12)

My bias is that this is one of the best verses in all of scripture. In the afternoon of the first garden, Father God sought for sweet fellowship with Adam and Eve. But they were hiding, as we tend to. We hide from the love of God, our friends and neighbors, and from ourselves. Hiding is the only answer we see for us. It develops a pretentious lifestyle within us. We find some shelter which stifles our growth.

In the garden of God's presence, our fellowship is broken. We broke it and He restored it. There is a garden within us which draws His presence. He loves this place! He loves both the beauty and His precious fellowship within us.

It is a place in which we enjoy His personal living word. It is not a place into which we invite our world. It's far too noisy! This garden is that special place of life-giving intimacy. He in me and I in Him, intimate and personal.

> You shall no more be termed forsaken, and your land
> shall no more be termed desolate; but you shall be called
> My delight is in her, and your land Married; for the
> Lord delights in you, and your land shall be married.
> —Isaiah 62:4

A great need in the body of Christ is to open the ear of our hearts for this quality of fellowship with the living God. Most Christians are not aware of this possibility and believe they are not good enough to deserve it.

The woman from the dark tents simply cried out for this intimacy. She certainly did not earn it or deserve it. But she did receive it! And a group traveled with her who had not received it.

We are in that crowd. But that's not His desire for us. Intimacy, that's where He's at, kissing intimacy drawing us as close as possible, with us loving it. That's where it's at!

(See Psalm 89:14–18, 116:7.)

"Make haste my beloved, and be like a gazelle or a young stag upon the mountains of spices" (8:14)

There is One who knows my heart more than any other. And in spite of this He calls me "My love." In drawing me ever closer He births within me a deeper response to Him as "my beloved." These two informal responses create within me a fresh depth of life and understanding as to who I am for eternity.

> Oh, precious Savior of my soul, and far more;
> Precious Bridegroom of my heart, and far more;
> Merging your fullness of grace and beauty into my
>   brokenness, and far more, much more;
> Beautiful King of glory, and still much, much more;
> Draw me after You and I will run!
> Draw me far beyond all that I perceive that I am.

> *I know that I am asking according to your beautiful heart, because You inspired this song. And it is to captivate my heart. Your plan for me is great and wonderful! Thank You for choosing me long before I was ever able to choose You. Amen, selah, and hooray!*

"Make haste my beloved" (8:14)

> *Father God, and great Lover of my soul, I suspect there is no other structure on earth that You prefer to be housed in than this form of the human heart. I also sense I don't begin to understand the fathomless depth within Your heart which passionately connects in You. You are at home in me. Your unique fullness of life is fully at rest in me.*

> *The human heart desperately needs new birth to reconnect. And we go through life sensing this disconnect yet not perceiving that it's all about You. You describe it as being lost. Indeed we are lost and live out our lives in that precise condition.*

So, right now, fill my life with Your kisses of the mouth, for Your love is sweeter than wine and Your anointing oils are fragrant, rightly do the maidens love You.

Calling us in You as Your bride is truly not as preposterous as we might believe. So do it and keep doing it: call me bride. Your kisses represent this quality of union in heaven's Bridegroom love.

"O let him kiss me with the kisses of his mouth. Your love is sweeter than wine, your anointing oils are fragrant" (1:2).

You insist on loving me on Your terms! Release all that I am into Your calling on my life, which involves being kissed by You! This quality of revelation holds me in Your presence! Amen.

To Contact the Author

VHELWEG@GMAIL.COM

Notes

INTRODUCTION

1. Watchman Nee, *The Song of Songs* (London: Christian Literature Crusade, 1966), 11.

SONG ONE
CHAMBER LOVE

1. St. Bernard of Clairveaux, *On the Song of Songs I,* Volume 2 (Kalamazoo, MI: Cistercian Publications, 1976), 4.

2. Watchman Nee, *The Song of Songs*, 22.

3. J. Hudson Taylor, *Union and Communion* (Minneapolis, MN: Bethany Fellowship, n.d.), 29.

4. Charles Spurgeon, "A Bundle of Myrrh," Sermon #558, delivered Feb. 28, 1864.

SONG FOUR
POWER AND GLORY

1. Watchman Nee, *The Song of Songs*, 159.

2. J. Hudson Taylor, *Union and Communion*, 72.

3. Watchman Nee, *The Song of Songs*, 165.

4. St. Bernard of Clairveaux, *On the Song of Songs*, 6–7.

SONG FIVE
GLORIOUS UNION

1. J. Hudson Taylor, *Union and Communion*, 80.